The Private Journal Of The Marquess Of Hastings: Edited By His Daughter The Marchioness Of Bute. In Two Volumes...

The marquess of Hastings

THE
PRIVATE JOURNAL

OF THE

MARQUESS OF HASTINGS,
K.G.

PRIVATE JOURNAL

OF THE

MARQUESS OF HASTINGS,

K.G.

Governor-General and Commander-in-Chief in India.

EDITED BY HIS DAUGHTER,

THE MARCHIONESS OF BUTE.

IN TWO VOLUMES.

VOL. I.

LONDON:
SAUNDERS AND OTLEY, CONDUIT STREET.
1858.

LONDON:

SAVILL AND EDWARDS, PRINTERS, CHANDOS-STREET,

COVENT-GARDEN.

PREFACE.

FRANCIS, second Earl of Moira, afterwards created Marquess of Hastings, was appointed to the government of British India in the early part of 1813, which post He held for nine years. He was constituted both Governor-General and Commander-in-Chief by His own solicitation, not from an overweening love of power, but because He felt that under the then anxious state of Indian affairs, it would be impossible for Him to carry out His views of duty to His country with a divided authority; and He therefore stipulated, before He accepted the appointment, for the labour and responsibility of both offices. Nor was it from mercenary motives that He grasped at this lofty posi-

tion, for He omitted to make any terms as
to remuneration, and He yielded the question
of adequate recompence when He found it
was arranged that the salary of Governor-
General only was to be assigned to Him, satisfied that the concentrated power gave Him
additional means of usefulness. Even when
in the field, at the head of the army, He
did not receive the allowances of a general
officer on active service. The East India
Company, however, afterwards acknowledged
their sense of His services by bestowing on
His family two grants of money, in sums of
60,000*l.* and 20,000*l.* respectively.

But this pre-eminence was wisely obtained
at any sacrifice; and the Almighty merci-
fully bestowed the bodily vigour, which
enabled Him at His advanced age, for so
many years, to maintain an unremitting
exertion of mind which none of His suc-

cessors (save Lord William Bentinck for a short time) have since attempted: for at an interesting period of Anglo-Indian history, Lord Hastings was capable of controlling the extensive machinery at one glance, and in this Journal He has noted many of the principles that guided Him. At a time like the present, when India absorbs so much general attention, it may be not only interesting, but useful to observe the impressions received even forty-five years since, by a man of mature age, of experience in life under various phases, and whose position afforded him an unlimited insight into all points, both civil and military, of this vast Eastern Empire.

This Journal was written for the purpose of recording for His children's information the principles upon which He acted. It is therefore strictly copied from the original

MS., even to the very words; though the changes which are constantly obtaining in our language, tend to throw a look of antiquity and obscurity over what was in Lord Hastings' time polished English. It is only curtailed as to the voyage, then of six months' duration, and now so well known that the details would be tedious; and some of the accounts of hunting expeditions are left out, as the too frequent recital of such scenes might prove wearisome to strangers. It will be observed, that Lord Hastings abruptly concluded His Journal in December, 1818, though His government of India continued to January, 1823. He probably found that it was impossible to keep it with the immense labour of the ordinary duties of His double office, which, Lord William Bentinck, who for some months performed the same, expressed his astonishment that Lord Hastings' health and strength could stand for so many years. The following passage in his common-place book shows the opinion Lord Hastings entertained of the usefulness of first impressions, and which He held even after He had left India. "Though it would not immediately suggest itself, reflection may excite the surmise that a person who comes newly into a country is likely to form a more just notion of its political position than others who have continually resided in that realm; the circumstances menacing its quiet having advanced upon the latter so gradually, as not to have roused apprehension by their growth, and being too familiar to suggest in their matured state due considerations of their tendency and importance."

It may be matter of surprise to some that, if worth publishing now, this Journal was not given earlier to the public; but there are many who feel as Walpole did respecting his biography, that personal narrations may come too near a public man's contemporaries; and till latterly India has not been a source of public interest, inquiry being mainly confined to those connected with the country. Lord Hastings' daughters have, from these motives therefore, withheld the papers bequeathed to them until now: and the survivor of those "Companions of his Expedition" to whom He affectionately dedicates His Diary, which has been found in the arrangement of the mass of His papers, has only lately decided on the publication of her Father's "Private Journal," believing there are still many who will gladly recall in these pages the sentiments they have heard Him express when in life.

DEDICATION.

———

THIS Journal is undertaken for the sake of the Dear Little Companions of my Expedition. It will be both gratifying and useful to them in a future day to have their recollection of circumstances revived, and to have many matters explained which they will be likely to have comprehended but imperfectly. At any rate, it will convince them of the solicitude felt for them by a fond Father.

THE

PRIVATE JOURNAL

OF

THE MARQUESS OF HASTINGS.

The Earl of Moira embarked at Portsmouth, on board H.M.S. *The Stirling Castle*, under command of Admiral Sir Home Popham, accompanied by the Countess of Loudoun and Moira, and his three eldest children, on the 14th of April; and landed at Madras on the 11th of September, 1813.

September 11th.—Made the land near Sadras at daybreak. Ran along the coast, and anchored in Madras roads about twelve o'clock. The admiral, Sir Samuel Hood, and the staff-officers of the Presidency, came aboard to visit me. Soon after the admiral had retired, the Governor-General's flag (the union at the main topmast-head) was hoisted and was saluted by the admiral's ship and the other king's ships in the roads as well as by the fort. At five we left the ship, and landed amid a prodigious concourse of people. The first view was very striking. The notion of population conveyed by the immensity of the crowd, together with the novelty of the dresses and the tranquil demeanour of the individuals amid excessive pressure, marked to one's perception a state of society altogether different from what we had been accustomed to contemplate. The surf appeared insignificant, and the artifice of the native boatmen (who rowed us in a Massoulah boat) to make it be thought of consequence, was easily seen through. Without doubt it is at times dangerous, as is the case in all tropical countries where there is a flat shore. I repaired through a double line of troops, passing across the fort to the Governor's house. There the judges and principal officers of the Presidency were introduced to me by Lieutenant-General Abercromby, who united for the time the functions of Governor and Commander-in-Chief. I thence went to the Ameer Baugh, which had been prepared for our reception. It is a garden palace built by the Nawab of the Carnatic, at a period when the situation was retired and when he could make a variety in his mode of life by coming to it occasionally as a retreat. Now that country seats or villas are built all around it, there can be no temptation for the Nawab ever to visit it; on which account the Government has *borrowed* it of him, as a residence to be applied to the reception of the Governor-General whensoever he repairs to Madras. Servants hired by the Government were ready to attend us. The house is handsome and convenient, and the situation is as pleasant as one in a dead flat can be. Trays of fruit from the Nawab, with a letter of congratulation on our arrival, were ushered in in great form. I wrote a civil note of acknowledgment, which I afterwards understood was regarded as a particular politeness. It seemed to me that the returning a verbal compliment, or the making a secretary write on the occasion, would be a great deficiency in breeding. After dressing, we went to dine at the Governor's. All the principal ladies and gentlemen of the Presidency were there.

September 12th, Sunday.—Went to divine ser-

vice in the fort, The church is decorous, and the
service was becomingly performed. After church,
I received the judges and council at the Ameer
Baugh. Wrote by express to Lord Minto. Dined
with the Governor, a private party. Heard the
details of the contest then raging for precedence
between the daughters of peers and the wives of
those who, from their station in the Company's
service, were held to have a superior local rank.
As the affair had been referred to the Governor-
General in Council, I had not to give any opinion
upon it; and a hope which I was told had been
entertained that I should indirectly decide the
question by my choice of the lady whom I should
hand out at this dinner was baffled by my adverting laughingly to the dispute while I gave one
arm to Lady Hood (Lord Seaforth's daughter),
and the other to Lady Strange, the wife of the
Chief Justice.

September 13th.—The Governor came to me
after breakfast, and we went in minute detail
through the state of the Presidency. I found him
not at all easy respecting the dispositions of the
army, which he regarded as sullen, though not

inclined to immediate outrage. I remarked that such a temper was not surprising when nothing had been done to soothe the dissatisfactions remaining after tho late convulsion; since which period the army, conscious of its own anxiety to return to its duty, had been left to feel itself as only resting under an ungracious pardon. It was recommended by me that every opportunity should be seized to cheer the officers and reanimate their honest pride.

Lieutenant-General Abercromby observed that my commissions implied a more continued and active intervention of the Governor-General with the other Presidencies than had hitherto existed; that it was what he had expected; and that the utility of such a connexion was in every view of public interest unquestionable. He said that the Nawab of the Carnatic had sent to express to him (the Governor) a hope that I would pay his Highness the first visit, as had been done by Lord Cornwallis and Lord Minto; but that he had answered his Highness, it was what he could not mention to me, as he was sure that, from the particular ground on which I stood, I must expect the

Nawab to wait upon me. This the Governor said
he had taken upon himself to determine, in consequence of my having the day before explained to
him my purpose of holding up the Government at
Calcutta with more form and state than had heretofore been maintained; a resolution which he
strongly encouraged, professing his conviction that
such a tone would be no less agreeable to individuals
than useful in its influence on public concerns. He
said the present procedure towards the Nawab
appeared to him essential from the impression it
would make on the natives. I agreed perfectly
with him.

After the Governor was gone, we had a party of
jugglers for the amusement of the children. Their
deceptions, though well managed, were not so
striking as their skill in balancing and their extraordinary precision in throwing up and catching a
number of balls in rapid rotation. For both these
last achievements it seems necessary that the attention of the performer should be aided by the cadence
of a song which his comrades chant to him with
great earnestness. One trick merits investigation.
The juggler put a small ball into his mouth, whence

smoke immediately issued. Soon after, he blew out flame strong enough to consume flax at a little distance. The ball must have been of the phosphorus which ignites with moisture. But the retaining it in the mouth after it was inflamed depends on a secret worthy of being ascertained.

I had some of the staff and other officers to dine with me. Our table was as regularly conducted as if our household had been established for a year. I notice this to do justice to the attention and activity of the native servants, by whom alone everything was managed. An equal number of English servants, unaccustomed to act together, could not have been tutored to fulfil their business with similar accuracy.

September 14th.—Rode out immediately after gun-fire. I observed great numbers of the date-palm, and casually asked if the dates were good. It was answered that the trees here never produced any fruit. Can this be owing to the ignorance of the natives that male palms must be planted among the others to make the latter fruitful? I have spoken on the subject with several of the natives in the course of the morning, as well as with some of the oldest white inhabitants, and none of them had a notion that male palms were requisite for the fecundity of the date-tree. As all the plantations on the Choultry plain have been made within these thirty years, and there is no tree of spontaneous growth in that tract, it is possible that it may have been thought unadvisable to plant a tree which had been remarked as never yielding fruit. The rendering the date-trees in the vicinage of Madras prolific would be a great benefit to numbers of the lower classes; therefore I shall solicit Governor Farquhar to forward to Madras some young male palms from the botanic garden at the Isle of France. The dates, which are now consumed in considerable quantity at Madras, are all imported from Bussorah.

At eleven I had a levee; after which I received several individuals who had letters to me or particular applications to make. In the afternoon I began the study of various plans submitted to the Government for the constitution of the army and for the defence of the territory. These plans are entered on the records; and what related to position was explained by the Quartermaster-General's map.   Dined at home with some of the officers of the ship and some persons particularly recommended to us.

September 15th.—Went, as soon as it was light, to the fort, in order to inspect the works and to enable myself to judge of the system of exterior fortification proposed for the black town. The drawings had been shown to me the day before by Major-General Trapand, the chief engineer. Fort St. George is a very respectable fortress, such as ought to sustain a long siege could a regular army sit down before it. Everything was in excellent condition. The water in the tanks, of which there is six months' supply for 10,000 men, is remarkably transparent and sweet, though it is said to have been in the tanks above thirty years. This resource is necessary, lest an enemy should discover and cut off the pipes by which water is brought to the Fort from a considerable distance.

At eleven I received the visit of the Nawab, who came in great state, and dressed out with a profusion of jewels. I met him at the door, and, on his stepping from his carriage, embraced him, according to the etiquette, four times, giving three

embraces to each of the three sons and the nephew
whom he introduced to me. I led him upstairs,
our arms being over each other's shoulders, while I
gave my left arm to the eldest son. On a sofa
drawn to the middle of the room I made him take
his seat to the right, placing myself next to him,
and seating the eldest son on my left. On another
sofa not so much advanced sat the other three
princes. The Company's Persian secretary had a
chair close in front of the Nawab and me, so as
that he might interpret between us without being
overheard by our respective attendants, who formed
a circle around.

The conversation began by compliments—hopes
that I and my family had not suffered by the length
of the voyage, and inquiries relative to the King
and the Prince Regent. He then adverted to the
treaty, and professed his anxiety for an assurance
that I should cause its provisions to be observed.
I had been told that he had been under great alarm
lest I should still further degrade his already abject
condition; an apprehension probably entertained
from his knowledge that (when the vacancy of the
musnud was impending) application had been made

to me in favour of the unfortunate young man set aside by our Government to make way for this individual. I answered that a treaty plighted the public faith of the nation, so that it must be my duty to maintain its terms according to their true spirit, which ought always to be construed most favourably for the party whose sole dependence was on the honour of the other. He did not attempt to conceal his gratification at this answer. After some desultory conversation, he said I had too much business to make it proper for him to trespass longer on me. I then called for otto of roses and rose-water, with which I perfumed his handkerchief, gave him pawn—the prepared betel and areca nut—and threw round his neck a chaplet of rose-coloured odoriferous flowers. This ceremony I had been instructed to perform without rising from my seat; a point to which the Government here attaches much importance. I went through the same ceremony to the elder son. Then the three other princes were made to rise, and come up to me for the same compliment, the Nawab being particular in calling to each of them to make his obeisance in receiving it.

The chaplets provided for them were, according to rule, of only white flowers. We descended the stair in the original form. After I had embraced the Nawab at the carriage-door, he took hold of both my hands, and stooping very low, placed his head between them, desiring the Persian secretary to explain, that by that act he threw himself and family under my protection. This was a gesture not indifferent for the native crowd who witnessed it; yet I know not if it did not excite in me much more lively sensations, from the reflection on the altered state of that family through its adherence to British interests. The cavalcade departed with a rapid reiteration of " How d'ye do, Governor-General?" from all the great personages. Subsequently the Nawab told the Persian secretary that he had never been so happy in his life as my expressions respecting the treaty had made him. He expatiated, with effusions of gratitude, on my tone of politeness, which appeared to me no more than the simple due of humanity towards a family so grievously humiliated by us.

I then received a number of officers and others who had come from the neighbouring stations to see me.   After which I had another discussion on public business with the Governor.   We drove out near sunset to see a part of the environs.   The remarkable want of space in the residences of the natives, constructed principally of palm-leaves, irresistibly evinces the little hope there is that an open trade would find any market for those minor luxuries which form the principal article of British manufacture.   The Governor, members of Council, judges, and their ladies, with some other distinguished individuals of the Residency, dined with us.

September 16th.—Set out at dawn of day to review on the open ground in front of the fort the troops stationed at Madras.   Very heavy rain had fallen in the night, accompanied by much lightning, during which the jackals were loudly clamorous in our garden.   As those animals are rather useful in destroying minor vermin and carrion, they meet with little annoyance from either whites or natives.   The morning was fine; the ground had been improved by the wet.   The line consisted of the King's 89th regiment, five battalions of sepoys, and a rifle corps, and the Governor's body-guard.   They were in perfectly good order.

Their deploying from column and changes of front were done with great regularity and precision. I seized this opportunity to address to the whole of the Madras army an order calculated to cheer its feelings and awaken its confidence.

At eleven I went, according to appointment, to return the Nawab's visit. The preparation for our reception was in all the style of barbaric pomp, and exhibited what I suppose has been always the case with Asiatic magnificence, the oddest mixture of splendour and squalid destitution.

On entering the gate, the guard-houses, and other lodgments for attendants, presented themselves in the shape of wretched hovels. All his guards, horse and foot, were drawn out. The foot fell sadly short of our sepoys—whom they had daily before their eyes—and whom they obviously imitated in discipline as well as dress. The horse looked better, yet still with immeasurable inferiority of appearance to the body-guard which attended me. The whole saluted, lowering their standards. Four elephants and six camels were drawn out, decorated with gaudy trappings, and striking from richness as well as novelty. Close to these a mass of naked palankeen-bearers offered a singular contrast. There was not less discrepancy in the music. The breathings of a very soft kind of flute were curiously interrupted by the braying of a coarse sort of trumpet, and the rattle of most discordant drums. The Nawab met me at the door of his durbar. After the ceremony of embraces, I entered the hall, when His Highness begged that he might introduce the principal Mahomedan sirdars to me. They were chiefly respectable and modest-looking individuals, to whom I showed as much courtesy as the occasion would admit.

He then led me to the sofa, placing me on the left (the place of honour with them), and seating himself in the middle, with his eldest son on the right. My suite were placed on chairs in a semi-circle to the right. Some attendants stood behind the sofa. The other Moslems sat on low cushions close to the wall of the durbar on either side, and by the uniformity of their white muslin robes, made an advantageous show. A glass door flanked our sofa. The curtain which covered it on the inside was every moment partially withdrawn; so that I imagine the Begum and other women were

gratifying their curiosity.   The Nawab said that
the expressions I had used to him the day before
had been balm to him; for that in his situation,
he must unavoidably be anxious upon every change
in the Government.   He requested that I would
look at the letters which he had received from the
King and the Court of Directors on his accession
to the musnud, as well as at one from Lord Cornwallis.   Having perused them, I said that my
language had not been unweighed; for, that the
existence of a specific treaty would have bound me
to strict observance of what I found so settled, even
had the greatest political difference reigned between
me and those who made the arrangement.   I felt
pledged to that principle of duty, and to the fulfilment of its true spirit of personal honour.   He
appeared overjoyed, and asked whether I wished to
have his two sons under my eye at Calcutta, as
Lord Cornwallis had had the children of Tippoo.
I answered, that the case was widely different between a vanquished enemy and the representative
of a family which had always preserved the most
faithful alliance; and added, that nothing should
induce me ever to give a colour for others to imply

a doubt which I myself could not for an instant entertain.   Learning that our departure was fixed for seven o'clock on Saturday morning, he insisted on attending us at the beach, and seeing us embark.

There was no controlling this resolution, though I resisted it as much as possible.

When I proposed to take my leave, he went through the ceremony which I had performed to him, hanging round my neck a long chain composed of Arabian jasmine, with red roses at intervals strung on silk, elegant as well as fragrant.   To Sir Home Popham and the other gentlemen who accompanied me, he gave white chaplets, with the compliment of pawn and rose water.   As we retired through the hall, he led me up to a full-length portrait of the Prince Regent, telling me that he knew the Prince and I had lived for years as brothers, therefore he was gratified in showing to me the picture.   At the door the embraces were repeated; and I departed with a peal of " How d'ye do, Governor-General?"

To my conception nothing can be more uncomfortable than the situation of this man.   Had he the spending of his vast income in the unshackled

independence of a private individual, the varied
enjoyments of life would be at his command; but
his character of a sovereign prince, shorn of every
exercise of power, subjects him to perpetual misre-
presentation amid a crowd of listless and unemployed
attendants; whilst its pretensions (capable of being
dangerously applied) oblige the British Government
to maintain a vigilance over him, which restricts
him from many innocent relaxations. The sports
of the field and change of place might give some
relief in the vacuity of his life; yet in these he
cannot indulge himself without a previous assent,
difficult to attain even after slow and discouraging
negotiation. The magnificence of his establishment, therefore, appeared to me only lamentable;
inasmuch as its natural consequence was to make
the grievousness of his position more sensible. On
quitting the Nawab's palace, I dismissed part of
the guards, with all the Chobdars and Peons, and
then returned, at the admiral's house on Choultry
Plain, the visit which Sir Samuel Hood had made
to me in the *Stirling Castle*. Reaching home, I
found a prodigious dinner sent (as is the form when
the Governor visits Chepauk Palace) from the

Nawab. I was of course under the necessity of looking at it and admiring it; and to say the truth the dishes seemed well-dressed, and in remarkably good condition, considering the distance they had come. Having made a present to the persons who had the charge of it, I caused the dinner to be divided among the sepoys of my guard, and the other natives in attendance. They appeared to relish it prodigiously.

I dined with the Governor at a public entertainment given in the banqueting-room. This is a building detached from the Government House. One of the temples at Athens furnished the plan. The edifice is handsome, and the interior constitutes a very fine room; but this heavy inconvenience attends it, that there is no apartment where the guests can wait while the dinner is preparing. The only remedy is to conceal the table by a screen, in front of which the company waits close to the entrance till it is time to sit down. The entertainment on this occasion was splendid.

At ten at night Lady Loudoun had a drawing-room, at which all the ladies and gentlemen were presented according to the formulary of Dublin

Castle. This had been previously arranged, to the great satisfaction of all the leading persons, who much applauded our intention of putting the Government of Calcutta on this high footing. The Governor, and all those the most intimate with us, were formally introduced, which made the ceremony appear quite regular to those not capable of appreciating the real utility of its purpose. Such persons might otherwise have thought the form ostentatious.

September 17th.—Saw another company of jugglers, which I mention in order to notice what they told us respecting the posture children attending them, by whom the strangest distortions of frame were exhibited. We were told that they began to subject the children to these dislocations when they are but a few weeks old. One would have supposed that such violence would have been fatal to an infant. The letting down the blade of a sword into, and beyond the stomach (performed before us) is no deception. It is an unpleasant sight, as the performer obviously suffers pain. It is only in the senility of society that these devices are imagined; and this trick has accidentally survived the convul-

sions occasioned by the irruption of the Tartars;
an era decisive against the further progress of that
unprofitable ingenuity which lulled the dotage of
Hindoo civilization.

This morning I saw several officers from neighbouring stations.

At one, I received the visit of the Rajah Vasa-
reddy Vencatadry Naido. Part of his estates are at
Masulipatam, and the other part in the Guntoor
Circar. As a zemindar, he pays to the Company
annually nearly two lacs and a half of pagodas.
Having had permission to make a religious pilgrimage to Ramascocram, he wished to pay his
respects to the Governor of Fort St. George in his
way back. On his visit, he presented two elephants
and four camels. A present to him being requisite
in return, by some strange mistake his own elephants and camels were sent to him on the part of
the Company. The poor man was in despair at
a procedure which, he said, was to disgrace him for
ever in the eyes of his people; to heal this wound
I agreed to receive him. I stipulated that his present to me should be very small, as no return could
be made for it, and as I should pay him the com-

pliment of accepting it, instead of merely putting
my hand on it, and restoring it. He came with a
strange motley attendance of armed men, which
my Moslem servants censured as an improper
assumption of state. In this hottest day of the
hottest month at Madras, he was wrapped in a
robe of green velvet. The pearls and emeralds
which he wore were fine. He presented a white
handkerchief, folded and highly perfumed, with two
oranges, and three or four dozen of small gold
coins on it. I directed the interpreter (having
first taken it into my own hand) to transmit it to
the Company's secretary; and I made the Rajah
sit on the sofa with me. His manner appeared
very polished. After thanking me for the favourable reception, he asked my leave to make a pilgrimage to Benares; which I readily granted. He
then rose to depart; but I made him stop till I
poured some rose-water on his hands, for which he
expressed much gratitude. The Moslems told some
of my gentlemen that it was too much civility
towards a Hindoo. I had the satisfaction of thinking that the poor Rajah's respectability was restored
in his own contemplation, and that of his followers.

Soon after his departure, I received all the native officers of the several corps in the neighbourhood. This was novel; but it was a step taken after full deliberation between me and Governor Abercromby. The recent conspiracy of some native officers against their white superiors in sepoy regiments suggested the measure. I addressed them through an interpreter; applauded their experienced fidelity; explained that in no course of things could they meet so sure a reward for their services as under the settled dominion of the Company; and assured them of my disposition to uphold the respectability of their present situations, as well as to make their retirement (when age should require it) distinguished and comfortable. They appeared much pleased.

At four o'clock, I had a review of the artillery at St. Thomas's Mount. The weather was intensely hot; yet the corps, both horse and foot, displayed itself most creditably. In the essentials for service, it is not at all inferior to the royal artillery. In the meantime, Lady Loudoun paid a visit to the Begum. The brocade and shawls given on this occasion by the Begum to the children and Lady

Loudoun were sent by the latter to the Company's secretary, it being her resolution so to act with regard to any presents she may receive while in this country.   On my return from St. Thomas's Mount, I encountered a prodigious dinner, sent by the Begum to Lady Loudoun.

We satisfied the bearers, and gratified the appetites of all the natives around us.

Dinner awaited us at the admiral's.   It is rare that a magnificent entertainment is a pleasant one; but Sir Samuel and Lady Hood had the talent to make this so.   After the dinner there was a ball, at which we stayed to a very late hour.

September 18th.—Rose, after being in bed an hour and a half; and, despatching what business remained to be arranged at the Ameer Baugh, repaired to the Governor's.   There I met the members of Council, and we had a short recapitulation of points that had received previous discussion.

Thence we proceeded, through the fort, between two lines of the troops to the beach, where Lady Loudoun was to meet us.   At a tent pitched for the purpose, I met the Nawab and his sons.   On Lady Loudoun's arrival, he gallantly handed her into the boat, and was particular in taking leave of my son. He begged me to notice that he had stationed his artillery lower down the beach, the jurisdiction of the fort not permitting its near approach, to salute the flag of my boat as soon as it should put off from the shore. Our embraces were renewed. After I got into the boat, he came to the side; and, taking my hands, placed his head between them, saying that I knew what it meant. We pushed through the surf without inconvenience, yet with occasion to observe that there was dexterity in our boatmen. On reaching the ship, I found a present of one hundred baskets of fruit from the Nawab. The boon was very acceptable, as its extent enabled me to send a portion to every mess of the sailors.

There were some baskets of oranges from Hyderabad, of peculiarly good quality, and of a kind I had never seen before. They are remarkably thin-skinned, and have a little bitter tinge in their flavour, which renders their sweetness less luscious. As the Nawab perceived that there was not a breeze to enable us to put to sea, he exhibited a quantity of rockets for our amusement (from a pleasure house which he has upon the shore) as soon as

it was dark.   This shows the sedulity of attention
with which the natives court you when they have
any point of interest to carry.   A fine breeze sprang
up about nine o'clock.   We weighed anchor, and
soon lost sight of the ships in the road, carrying
with us a very cordial feeling towards Madras.

September 24th.—Just at sunset we made the
land at False Point, but saw no pilot-vessel.
Finding the water shoal, stood off till towards
morning, firing guns and throwing up rockets occasionally.

September 25th.—About the middle of the day
we were in Balasore road; discovering no vessel
in that quarter, we stood eastward for the Sand
Heads.   Late in the afternoon the *Hastings* pilot-
vessel came to us.

The pilot would not carry us over the Sands this
evening, as it was becoming dark; therefore we
came to anchor.

September 26th, Sunday. — Weighed in the
morning, and ran across the two Sands.   There
not being sufficient breeze for us to stem the ebb,
we anchored in the Eastern Channel; and I despatched Major Doyle, with Major Macleod, to give

Lord Minto information of my approach. They went in a small vessel, capable of going over all the shallows; but they did not make much way from us.

September 27th. — Got under sail with the change of tide, just before dawn. After a short time, the wind became directly adverse.

We continued to work up till the tide failed, when we anchored within distant view of Saugur Island.

September 28th.—With the tide we made a little progress, and at last anchored in Saugur road, about two miles from the shore, but abreast of the island. The land is so flat, so sandy, and so covered with a very tall silvery grass that it affords no temptation, even were the multitude of tigers by which it is infested out of the question. We got some fresh butter and some fine fish; the former brought down from Kedgeree, the latter caught in the roads.

September 29th. — Quitted the *Stirling Castle,* and embarked in the *Hastings* schooner. The wind was scant and feeble; and the flood tide was so weak, it being now the neap, that we made little way against the heavy body of water coming down the river. We were soon obliged to anchor, without having reached Kedgeree; abreast of which place we did not arrive till the middle of the night, with a new tide.

September 30th. — Excellent bread, eggs, and butter, with a jar of milk, were sent off to us by the post-master. Our progress this day was not more than four miles.

The heat was excessive; and the smallness of the vessel made our position very uncomfortable. The ladies and children, however, bore the inconveniences with the truest good humour.

October 1st.—Early in the morning, Sir W. Keir (King's adjutant-general), with Mr. Elliot and Lieutenant Allen, sent by the Governor-General, came aboard our vessel. They had hastened down the river in another pilot-vessel on hearing of our being in Saugur roads. They brought vegetables and refreshments of various kinds. They communicated the agreeable intelligence that the *Phœnix* yacht could not be far off, as she was to follow them with all expedition. In fact, we saw her by the middle of the day; and at three o'clock we got aboard her.

A remarkably well-dressed dinner was ready for us, with attendants from the Government House. In point of space and coolness, we had changed much for the better; but the myriads of cockroaches with which we were pestered formed no immaterial consideration in the opposite scale.

October 2nd.—With the night's tide we had got up as high as Diamond Harbour, where we had anchored among a number of the Company's and other ships. As soon as it was clear day, all the vessels appeared dressed out with as many flags as they could hoist, and saluted with their guns. Commodore Hayes and the Commander of one of the Company's cruisers came aboard, the former proposing to accompany us in his boat, and secure to us any assistance that might tend to accelerate the very slow progress we were making. We weighed anchor as soon as the tide would allow. Flat as are the banks of this river, they present objects very striking to an European eye unaccustomed to similar scenery. The forms of the trees, the appearance of the small, light-coloured cattle, and, above all, the frequent recurrence of the villages, attract one's attention forcibly. The habitations naturally excite an estimate of the people. Long residence in a country corrects a multitude of false notions hastily adopted respecting it; but, on the other hand, the mind becomes so familiarized with the habits of the people as to discard with its errors many remarks and discriminations made on its earlier view which would be better retained. Let me, therefore, define to myself the impression made on me by what I now see, divesting myself as far as is practicable of opinions gathered from reading, and figuring this people as contemplated for the first time. The survey is not favourable to the natives. True, the thickness of the population, and the extraordinary closeness with which the habitations are irregularly packed together, may afford unquestionable conclusion of the absence of those virulent passions which in other countries set hamlet against hamlet, and house against house. Vicinity of residence is impracticable where vehemence of temper would find unceasing ground of irritation and opportunity of jarring in eternal contact. Our towns are no contradiction to this statement; for the regular distribution of the houses along a neutral street, and the seclusion which the form of each dwelling affords to the family occupying it, counteract almost all the objectionable circumstances of proximity. In the Hindoo villages the dwellings are but three or four feet asunder; they are insulated, irregularly grouped as if by accident, and those which lie in the centre are approachable only by tortuous paths; and, as these habitations are simple huts, without exterior precincts, and are in part composed of mats pervious to sight, the possibility of the people's living in that huddled manner implies a destitution of those energies of mind on which moral feeling depends. Pudency cannot exist in such a crowded assemblage, notwithstanding the professed segregation of the women; and that state of society can be maintained only by reciprocal tolerance of all that is offensive and all that is indecent. The Hindoo appears a being nearly limited to mere animal functions, and even in them indifferent. Their proficiency and skill in the several lines of occupation to which they are restricted, are little more than the dexterity which any animal with similar conformation, but with no higher intellect than a dog, an elephant, or a monkey, might be supposed capable of attaining. It is enough to see this in order to have full conviction that such a people can at no period have been more advanced in civil polity. Retrogradation from an improved condition of society never takes this course. According to the circumstances which have dissolved its government the fragments of such a community either preserve the traces of effeminate refinement, or the rough fierceness stamped upon them by the convulsions amid which the centre of the fabric perished. Does not this display the true condition of India, and unveil the circumstances through which we have so unexpectedly and so unintentionally obtained empire here? There surely never has been an active and vigorous Hindoo population; nor are any of the bold, though rude, monuments of antiquity (as I think) ascribable to this race.

A confederacy of interested and forecasting sensualists, the Brahmins, conspired, when Hindoo society was young, to take care that its growth should be strictly in such a fashion as would ensure to them the continuance of those selfish advantages which their impositions on the multitude had obtained. Hence flowed all those inculcations which were to keep the frames and minds of the people in a state of feebleness adapted to the submission sought for them. They were taught to regard bathing in the Ganges as a religious duty, that by fixing themselves on its banks they might not escape the superintendence or the convenience of their spiritual guides, or be led to contemplate the examples of sturdier communities. They were instructed to marry in absolute infancy, that the energies of love might never rouse them to a consciousness of innate rights : and possibly the notion that debility of race would be entailed by this premature wedlock was no immaterial motive for its having been enjoined. They were bewildered in a variety of beliefs and infinity of observances (not maintained by their teachers themselves), that the listlessness of life might be filled by the multiplicity of factitious obligations, and that their intellects might never disentangle the intricacies of the creed imposed on them. They were interdicted from admitting proselytes, that no discussion of matters of faith might give their reason a clue towards emancipation. Everything in their system bears the stamp of successful conspiracy against human genius. That this portrait would not suit many of the tribes higher up the country I well know; but those tribes would not come within my notion of Hindoos, although they bear the name and have the appearance, and profess the religious tenets, of the Hindoos. One may confidently assume that India has in very remote periods, far anterior to the invasions recorded in annals or traditions, been the prey of the robust and hardy nations on its borders. A band of these conquerors, unlettered and devoid of hereditary pious practices, would care little what instruction was given to the children born to them by the Hindoo women whom they would collect in forming settlements within the regions they had subdued. The progeny thence assumed the name and the manners and the creed of the Hindoos; but with an elasticity of spirit drawn from the paternal stock. In those districts, therefore, the inhabitants, though assimilated in general semblance, and in the course of generations become enfeebled by the adopted habits, would not stand within the description of those communities which have remained fixed to the banks of the Ganges. It is of the latter I speak when I say I should think them, from the present frame of their polity, incapable of ever having effected or even undertaken anything on an extensive scale. The remnants of aught that was laborious in achievement or magnificent in plan may be satisfactorily assigned to the intruders who at several periods have held transitory dominion in different parts of India. These states have successively been subverted by new migratory hordes, the original Hindoos remaining indifferent to these revolutions. Hence there never has been a really national feeling among the people of this country. The great mass of the natives have no consideration of pride or other sentiment as to who governs them, provided their superstitions and nearly vegetative comforts be not outraged. The smaller and more active communities have no bond of union; Islamism itself having been prevented from becoming a cement by the animosities and incessant hostilities which have raged between the Moslem powers. An army, therefore, collected out of those broken sovereignties, if it be in number and discipline superior to what a confederacy of those intrusive chiefs can bring into the field, must rule India.

Amount and regularity of pay binds securely to our service the individual who has no other mode of subsistence but military engagement: and so recognised by that class of men are the advantages of being enrolled under the British standard, that there are few corps belonging to any of the native princes which would not come over to us on invitation, were our funds ample enough to answer for their maintenance. This security is to be understood as existing so long as we abstain from revolting the prejudices of the native troops. Men in all times have attached to trifling particularities an importance paramount to the most solid interests; and the disposition is perhaps more jealous on that head in this country than in any other. Under the name of intrusive chiefs I decidedly include the Mahrattas; a power comparatively novel, and formed originally by the aggregation of fugitives from the oppressions which have depopulated immense tracts that were subject to Mahomedan sway.

October 3rd.—We had brought-up in the night nearly off Myapore. The state boats had joined us at Diamond Harbour, but it was more conve-

nient to remain on board the yacht than to get into
them.   We made, however, so little way in the
course of this day, that in the evening we transferred ourselves to the *Sonamuckhee*, a beautiful
pleasure vessel, in order to be tracked up by men
collected for the purpose.   In this manner we were
towed along Garden Reach by moonlight.   The
elegance of the villas by that chastened light
was very striking.   We anchored off Mr. Kyd's
dockyard, about a mile short of Fort William.

October 4th.—We weighed anchor before dawn,
as I had given notice that I would land at six, in
order that the troops drawn out to receive me
might get back to their barracks before the sun
was high.   It was now the warmest and worst
part of the year; and this year the weather had
been more than ordinarily oppressive.   The heat
had been intense during our whole passage up the
river. The fort saluted as we passed.   We brought-
to off Chaudpaul Ghaut, our destined landing-place,
before six.   As soon as the clock struck that hour,
we got into the *Feel-cherry*, a highly ornamented
barge, and proceeded to shore.   Lady Loudoun
and the children were put into a carriage and

despatched to the private door of the Government House, whence she was conducted at once to her apartments. I walked with the general officers and staff, who met me at the ghaut, through the lane made by the 24th regiment and the sepoy battalions to the front of the Government House. Lord Minto, with all the gentlemen of the presidency, was waiting for me at the top of the magnificent staircase which leads to the entrance on that side. The appearance was very grand. After salutations, the gentlemen were confusedly presented to me in the outer hall. We then adjourned into the great hall, where breakfast was prepared. As soon as it was over, I was led to the council chamber, where my commission was read; and I then took the oaths and was invested with the charge of the Government. The completion of this ceremony was announced by the firing of the guns of Fort William. The crowd gradually dispersed. Lord Minto retired to a house which he had prepared in Chouringhee, a beautiful suburb of Calcutta. I was left to advert to domestic arrangements.

1814.

FEBRUARY 1st.—The excessive pressure of business immediately after my arrival, and the sacrifice of time unavoidable in giving audiences to individuals, prevented my continuation of the Journal. I am led to resume it now from frequent regret at not having minuted many transactions on the day of their occurrence, though even at present I feel all the difficulty of being able to adhere to the plan. The situation of a Governor-General, if he really fulfil his duties, is one of the most laborious that can be conceived. The short periods for the exercise indispensable to health, and for meals, can barely be afforded. There is, however, such peculiar advantage in recording one's opinions while they are fresh, with a view to one's future consideration or reference, that it must be attempted.   In resuming the task, I must advert briefly to what has occurred as most particular in the interval.

I have found the Government in a state of great

pecuniary embarrassment. The Directors were so urgent with me to send home treasure that I overcame the reluctance of my colleagues, and we remitted gold pagodas to the amount estimated by ordinary exchange of 300,000*l.* Should the price of gold in England be still what it was when I left Europe, this bullion will be sold by the Directors for not less than 450,000*l.* We have, however, in consequence been on the brink of great distress.

The embassy in Persia, though wholly appointed by the Crown, is entirely supported by the Government of Bengal; such being the arrangement made by ministers with the Directors, or rather imposed on the latter. Without any means of curbing the prodigality of the ambassador, or of determining the propriety of expenditures quite unconnected with the interests of India, we are bound to answer the bills drawn upon us by Sir Gore Ouseley. Of course they come both heavily and unexpectedly. The Governor of the Isle of France and the Governor of Ceylon have both had the privilege granted to them of drawing upon us, furnishing us in return with bills on the English Treasury, which we often cannot negotiate. Java is a still worse drain than

the others.   Instead of the surplus revenue which,
for the purpose of giving importance to the con-
quest, was asserted to be forthcoming from that
possession, it could not be maintained without the
treasury as well as the troops of Bengal.   Just
now, in the height of our exigencies, we receive an
intimation from the Lieut.-Governor that he cannot pay his provincial corps unless we allow him
50,000 Spanish dollars monthly in addition to the
prodigious sums which we already contribute to
his establishment.

Such is the condition in which I have found
finances.   The army, well disciplined, is insuf-
ficient in numbers for the ordinary defence of the
frontiers and for internal duties.   The escort of
treasure (produce of the land revenue) from the
several districts to Calcutta, requires incessant de-
tachments, and fairly wears out the troops.   This
service cannot be alleviated by the substitution of
the Burkendauzes, or armed police.   A trial of
this was made not a month ago.   The party was
surprised at night by a body of dakoyts, or gang-
robbers.   Two of the guard were killed, fifteen
wounded, and the treasure was carried off by the

banditti. At Calcutta there is no cavalry (so necessary for checking tumult in a populous city) but
the Governor-General's bodyguard of one hundred
and twenty-five men. Another troop does not
exist between Calcutta and Sultanpore, a distance
of about 600 miles. The whole of the district between the Hooghly and Ragojee Bhoosla's territories is totally devoid of troops and unprotected.
None can be spared to it from the pressing demands of other quarters. Yet it is from that frontier of the Rajah of Berar that an incursion of
Pindarries, who would find no opposition in tra-
versing part of his dominions, is most likely to be
made into our richest provinces. The aggregate of
the force which could be produced by the several
Pindarry leaders is estimated at 30,000, principally
cavalry. These are professedly freebooters. Their
occasional plunder of districts belonging to the
Rajah of Berar, the Nizam, and Dowlut Rao
Scindiah, which always takes place when their exactions from the petty independent states do not
answer their wants, are winked at. Those sovereigns have no sensibility for the sufferings of their
subjects. They only calculate the diminution which

their revenue may undergo, setting against that
loss the convenience of being able on the sudden to
take into their pay such a swarm of light troops
in case of any breach with this Government.   To
us the Pindarries are no eventual resource; for a
stipulation in their engagement is invariably an
unlimited right of plunder; an atrocity to which
no extremity could make us give countenance. Our
deficiency in point of numbers might be balanced
by the goodwill acquired from neighbouring powers
through our justice and moderation, whence we
might look to security against attack. I find
nothing of the sort. We are engaged in captious
bickerings with all around us.   On my taking the
reins of Government into my hand seven different
quarrels likely to demand the decision of arms were
transferred to me.   Of these Macherry, Rewah,
Sawunt-Warree, and Kurnool have required military operations. The results have been favourable: but, except in the case of Rewah, where it
was necessary to punish the Sainghur chiefs, who
had waylaid and massacred a party of our sepoys,
not one of these enterprises presents an object
which (putting the justice out of the question)

was worth the effort. The differences with the Scindian ameers relative to Cutch, with the Nepaulese Government, and with the King of Ava, have been amicably settled, in consequence of my having had time to apply remedies to the misunderstanding. From the force of any of those powers no serious long opposition was to be apprehended. The expense of preparation is a strong objection to these squabbles. A much more important consideration is that these paltry triumphs leave an inveterate spirit of animosity towards us in the breast of those whom we have overborne.

A rational jealousy of our power is not likely to excite half the intrigues against us which must naturally be produced by the wanton provocations which we have been giving on trivial subjects to all the States around us. With a degree of concert thus indistinctly fashioned, those States must be ready to start up into combination whenever they may see us occupied with an enemy capable of employing our forces for any time. It may not be long before such an enemy may exhibit himself. The terms of amity on which we at present stand with Runjeet Sing are no guarantee against those projects which his known dislike of us, and his confidence in his own strength, have probably made him revolve in secret. Having reduced all the other communities of the Sikhs beneath his sway, and having subjected all the other territories in his vicinity, he possesses a force which the turbulence of his disposition will impel him to use; and there is no field for its exertion but the part of the British dominions bordering on the Sutlej. Should the King of Ava, who conceives his armies to be irresistible, at the same moment invade Chittagong, the opposing those attacks at the two extremities of our empire must ungarnish our prodigiously extended flanks. Then, there would be an opening for all the vengeance of the petty States to which I have alluded, as well as for the rapacity of the Pindarries. Such a juncture might be the signal of general effort against us without any apparently adequate cause of war. We have not simply to look to the irritation of those whom we have actually scourged with nettles. Each sovereign must have brought the case home to himself, and must have secretly sympathized with the durbars which he saw insulted and humiliated.

The Nawab Vizeer imagined himself to have purchased exemption from these petty but galling vexations by the cession of a large part of his dominions—a cession made under the assurance of his being perfectly independent in what remained. We have been authoritatively interfering with all the minor concerns of his domestic rule, till we have driven him to a desperation which he proclaimed in open durbar. The Rajah of Berar, nominally our friend, has evinced repeatedly his hostile suspicion of us. The Nizam does not disguise his absolute hatred of us, though he is in shackles whence he cannot extricate himself. The Rajah of Mysore and the British Resident are engaged in a contest of mutual crimination. Scindiah is in the utmost difficulty to find means for keeping his army together, and nothing could be to him a temptation equal to the occasion of plundering our opulent provinces.

Ameer Khan, who wields Holkar's forces, is professedly inimical to us.

Holkar's dominions being exhausted, his army must ravage some other country, otherwise it will dissolve; and he is now negotiating with the Pindarries for a joint attack on Nagpore. This object, on a former occasion, was held so eventually injurious to us that Lord Minto raised an army to march (though under no obligation of a treaty) to protect the Rajah, and baffled the undertaking. I have not money (the Company having no credit in Calcutta) to equip an army even if I saw the policy, as Lord Minto did, of defending Nagpore. Yet I am aware of the possibility that apprehension might make the Rajah suggest to those who are threatening him, a more attractive object for their views by offering to join in an extensive combination for the invasion of our possessions.

In short, I see around me the elements of a war more general than any which we have hitherto encountered in India.

This formidable mischief has arisen from our not having defined to ourselves or made intelligible to the native princes, the quality of the relations which we have established with them.

In our treaties with them we recognise them as independent sovereigns. Then we send a resident to their courts. Instead of acting in the character of ambassador, he assumes the functions of a dictator; interferes in all their private concerns; countenances refractory subjects against them; and makes the most ostentatious exhibition of this exercise of authority. To secure to himself the support of our Government, he urges some interest which, under the colour thrown upon it by him, is strenuously taken up by our Council; and the Government identifies itself with the Resident not only on the single point but on the whole tenor of his conduct. In nothing do we violate the feelings of the native princes so much as in the decisions which we claim the privilege of pronouncing with regard to the succession to the musnud. We constantly oppose our construction of Mahomedan law to the right which the Moslem princes claim from usage to choose among their sons the individual to be declared the heir-apparent. It is supposed that by upholding the right of primogeniture we establish an interest with the eldest son which will be beneficial to us when he comes to the throne. I believe nothing can be more delusive. He will profess infinite gratitude as long as our support is useful to him; but, once seated, his subsequent attachment will always be regulated by the convenience of the day. He, too, will in his turn have to feel our interference in the succession as well as in minor instances. With regard to the latter it might be argued that some interest of the Company is always really involved. The simple existence of such an interest is not the true question. What should be considered, is, whether the matter be of a proximity or magnitude to make the prosecution of it desirable at the expense of the disgust and estrangement which you sow by the procedure.

If a willing obedience to the influence of our Government be deemed an essential point, all subordinate concerns ought to be indifferent.

February 2nd.—At Barrackpore, preparing for a short excursion above Kishnagur. Our elephants and horses were yesterday despatched to be in readiness on our arrival.

As the day furnishes nothing particular, I revert to circumstances of which I had omitted to make insertion at the time of their occurrence. Mr. Thomson, the private secretary, was one afternoon to come hither from Calcutta. His way lay through one of the narrow, crowded bazaars of the city. It happened to be one of the great Hindoo festivals. He met in the bazaar a prodigious concourse of people, before whom was borne on a sort of platform carried by men, a large image of one of the Hindoo deities splendidly gilt.

The persons around it were chanting hymns to it. The postilion, with the insolence which the natives invariably show when they are in the service of any European of high station, made no attempt to leave a passage for his countrymen, but whipped his horses and drove into the middle of the procession.

The men who carried the platform, in endeavouring to get out of the way of the carriage, were thrown into a deep gutter, and the gaudy image was broken into pieces. Mr. Thomson expected all the religious indignation of the crowd to burst upon him; but to his great astonishment, instead of venting abuse upon him or even on the postilion, the people only laughed heartily, and picked up the shattered fragments with apparent good-humour. The circumstance appears trifling, but it is strongly characteristic of the temper of the Hindoos, who could thus at once pardon the outrage from a conviction that an insult to them had not been intended.

We had a puppet-show for the amusement of the children. The figures are moved with much dexterity; yet here the extent of Hindoo genius is particularly marked. All the figures are disproportioned, having heads ten times too large for their bodies. I am assured that it is just the same in every one of the multitude of puppet-shows going about, and that there is not the slightest variation in the scenes exhibited. It seems as if the people were incapable of imagining anything new even in a matter of amusement.

February 3rd.—Went to Calcutta to close any business (independent of the council) which might be pending, before I should go to Kishnagur. Nothing material occurring I shall record a very curious exhibition which I saw sometime ago at Barrackpore. A man (naked except the cloth round his waist) stood upon a spring-board, holding, with his arms extended, in each hand a hoop no larger than that his head could just go through it. He first showed us what it was he meant to do, and the apparent impossibility of his succeed-

ing in the attempt made me particularly watchful
to detect any artifice by which he might seem to
have performed the feat without having really
achieved it. Making the board vibrate, he threw
himself up backwards, and came down on his
knees; his left arm was passed behind his head;
the hoop held in the right hand had been forced
through the left-hand hoop, so that the latter
slid up the right arm, which appeared shackled by
it, and the head was through the hoop held in the
right hand. The complicated movements required
to produce this position were done so rapidly that
there was no following them with the eye in the
short space of the man's turning in the air; but I
am positive there was no deception in the exhibition. It was displayed in broad daylight in the
open air.

Some visitors arriving, I requested the man to
repeat it, with which he complied. This man
rates himself very high, and will only perform
before persons of considerable rank. He displayed
some other feats of agility, such as leaping through
a noose little more than capable of slipping over
his body; and fixing his head, arms, and legs

through five holes, in a kind of net, suspended so high as that it required an active spring to reach it. These, though really curious, did not appear to me so dexterous as the first.

February 4th.—Council. I lodged the formal notification of its being my intention not to be present at the four councils next ensuing after this week. In my absence, the senior member takes the chair; but the proceedings of the council must be sent to me, and no article registered in them is valid till it is confirmed by my signature. A curious petition was delivered to me; the petitioner, a native, complained that the officiating Brahmins, at a Temple of Kali, near Moorshadabad, refused to sacrifice him, wherefore, as it was unlawful for him to put himself to death, he solicited that I would order the Brahmins to immolate him. A short time ago I had another petition from a man, who implored that I would order his head to be cut off, as he was in a state of hopeless penury.

February 5th.—Council. Heavy rain fell, without any storm of wind, which is very rare at this season. It is likely to be beneficial to our party, for the weather had become very warm, and it is supposed this downfall will produce cool air for some time. Received some baskets of apples from the Nawab Vizeer. They are brought from Persia, and it is surprising how fresh they came after that immense length of journey. They are sweet but insipid; their look, however, is good, and they are prized as a rarity.

February 6th.—Went to church, and immediately after the service returned to Barrackpore. Reviewing what I have written respecting the political state of this country, I think it well to sketch what appears to me the corrective for many existing embarrassments.

Our object ought to be, to render the British Government paramount in effect, if not declaredly so. We should hold the other States as vassals, in substance though not in name; not precisely as they stood in the Mogul Government, but possessed of perfect internal sovereignty, and only bound to repay the guarantee and protection of their possessions by the British Government with the pledge of the two great feudal duties.

First, they should support it with all their forces on any call. Second, they should submit their

mutual differences to the head of the confederacy
(our Government), without attacking each other's
territories, a few subordinate stipulations on our
part, with immunities secured in return to the other
side (especially with regard to succession), would
render the arrangement ample without complica-
tion or undue latitude.   Were this made palatable
to a few States, as perhaps it easily might, the ab-
rogation of treaties with the Powers who refuse to
submit to the arrangement would soon work upon
their apprehensions in a way that would bring them
at last within the pale of the compact.   The completion of such a system, which must include the
extinction of any pretension to pre-eminence in the
court of Delhi, demands time and favourable coin-
cidences.   While, on the other hand, the difficulties
bequeathed to me are imminent, and might break
upon me at any instant.   A new government
always produces some suspension in animosities.
I have endeavoured to improve the juncture by
courteous and conciliatory language to the native
Powers; and I do hope I may remove considerable
soreness.   As for the rest, fortune and opportunities
must determine; but it is always well to ascertain

to oneself what one would precisely desire had one
the means of commanding the issue.

February 7th.—Embarked at four in the morning at Pulta Gaut, in the *Feel-Cherry*, attended
by five other boats. Passed Chinsura about sunrise, and afterwards Hooghly. There are handsome
houses in each, which look upon the river and are
pleasing objects from it. Parts of the banks were
somewhat elevated. On these the villages were
picturesque; but generally the sides of the river
are flat and destitute of feature, of cheerfulness,
and even of appearance of fertility. There is,
however, no real want of tillage; for beyond the
margin over which the eye out of a low boat cannot
peer, the ground is said to be assiduously cultivated.
Crowds of people assembled in front of the villages
to look at us; and the women saluted us with a
sort of tremulous hooting which I might have
thought expressive of distaste had I not been fore-
warned that such was their complimentary expression of welcome. This is the sound which Dr.
Buchanan, by the aid of a lively fancy, describes as
indicative of a lascivious feeling, on the occasion
of his hearing it uttered when the idol was drawn

forth from the temple of Jugganauth; so readily do our prejudices impose on our perceptions. Assuredly, this singular noise does not imply anything like the intoxication of spirit which might be inferred from our hurra. At three o'clock we turned out of the main river into the Hurdum Nullah. At five we reached the Ruttna Gaut, where we were met by Mr. Paton, judge of the district, and Mr. Armstrong the collector. Our tents, dispatched in advance, were ready pitched here, about three hundred yards from the landing-place. The natives who had assembled in great numbers, had made a little avenue to the tents by fixing plantain trees in the ground on each side of the road. After a comfortable dinner which had been awaiting us, I went out to receive the zemindars who were desirous of presenting their nuzzurs. These consisted of money, live partridges, deer, hares, and a porcupine, or of fruit and vegetables. I touched the mohurs and rupees with my hand, which is declining them while you acknowledge the compliment; I accepted the birds and beasts for Barrackpore; and the fruits after I had waved my hand over them, became, according to established custom, a scramble for the multitude. No native, consistently with their principles, can retain for his own use that which he has tendered as a nuzzur, although it has been declined by the person to whom it was offered. The crowd, therefore, get the vegetables, and the money is divided among Brahmins. The porcupine, alarmed by the bustle, or deserted by the person who had hold of him, got away among the tents. He was easily surrounded, but not readily taken; for although the people had cloths to throw over him, I observed they were very cautious about touching the animal. There was reason for this, since the man who at length caught him exhibited two quills sticking in his arm. The quills have small barbs upon them, which make them more easily drawn from their socket in the skin of the porcupine than from the flesh into which they have been forced. Lieutenant Caldwell, who commanded the company of Sepoy Grenadiers attached as a guard to our tents and baggage, shot two alligators in his way from Barrackpore. Wishing to stuff the largest, ten feet long, he had it opened. In the stomach were found the bangles of a little girl whom the animal had of course devoured.   Such accidents occur frequently, and are little attended to by parents as far as relates to future precaution; though I am told they appear to feel acutely the loss of a child.

February 8th.—Marched from our encampment about five o'clock, and reached Kishnagur before nine.   Our route had been over a well-cultivated country, much resembling the flat extended plains of the northern part of Norfolk (only not stony), with an horizon of plantations and minor masses of wood round the villages.   The poor villagers met us at each hamlet with presents of kids, poultry, eggs, cakes, and vegetables.   In declining the offering, I not only was particular in causing thanks to be returned for the attention, but in preventing our native followers from converting the articles to their own use; which, without much vigilance, they would have done.   These people have no mercy for each other.   We took up our lodging at Mr. Paton's, a very neat bungalow, or rather house of a single floor, on a handsome lawn dotted with trees.   Among other articles at a good breakfast, there were some fresh-water whitings from the Jellinghy.   They much resembled the

sea whiting, but appeared to me decidedly better.
Mr. Paton mentioned to me a circumstance respecting the release of a prisoner which had given
him much gratification.   At Christmas, I had sent
a power to the judge of every zillah to pardon and
set free five of the convicts condemned to public
labour in chains, who might appear most deserving
of liberation.   Mr. Paton discharged, among
others, a man who had been made over to us on
our first receiving the district from the native
sovereign as guilty of harbouring dakoyts, and
thence sentenced to perpetual imprisonment.   The
hasty acceptance of such accusations under the
Mahomedan Government made this man's crimi-
nality very doubtful; yet he had been working in
irons ever since.   His joy at being released was
excessive; which he explained to Mr. Paton by
saying that now his family would be able to show
him funeral observances at his death.   It is very
strange that these acts of clemency, or any inquiry
into the conduct of the prisoners with a view to
relaxation in the case of those who appeared cor-
rected, are quite unprecedented.   In the case of
dakoyts (gang robbers by profession) lenity is of

difficult exercise; because multitudes of the cri-
minals have urged that their fathers and grand-
fathers were dakoyts—that they themselves were
bred up to the practice, and that they had no
other means of supporting themselves but returning to it should they be liberated. Add to
this, they are well fed and gently treated in their
bondage. Still there must occur many cases where
the merciful interposition of Government could not
but be well applied. We dined at the collector's
(Mr. Armstrong), on the bank of the Jellinghy.
It was the first stream of clear water I had seen
since my arrival in India. Hence it was a re-
freshing sight. We slept at Mr. Paton's.

February 9th.—Went before breakfast to see the
Company's plantation of timber-trees. It is a spot
of ground of nearly four hundred acres, very parkish
in appearance, there being some little wave of
ground, with handsome trees irregularly scattered,
and here and there a thick thorny brake. Spots
of the best soil are broken up for the young trees,
which seem to thrive well. The teak always has a
look of being blighted, from the peculiar quality of
its leaves and flowers, but it seems to grow rapidly

here.   At Barrackpore it is slow in its progress.

February 20th.—We rode to Kishnagur.   The
sun was uncommonly powerful from the moment
of its first rising, and our ride was excessively hot.
The inhabitants of the several villages which we
passed had all collected to see us.   I observed that
their air was not merely respectful, but that there
was a kindness in it which could only be referred
to their satisfaction with the Government under
which they lived.   In truth, the people who visit
Calcutta from the dominions of any of the native
princes are astonishingly struck with the security
against oppression and the impartial distribution of
justice enjoyed by our subjects : and the latter, from
comparing notes with the strangers, are highly
sensible of their own advantages.   We took up
our quarters at the magistrate's as before.   We
could nowhere have met more frank, polite, and
unaffected hospitality.   Our party was here to
break up.   It had consisted of Major Stanhope,
Mr. Ricketts, Major Macleod, Major Forssteen,
Hon. W. Moore, Capt. Stanhope, Capt. Matthews,
Major Gordon, Deputy-Adjutant-General, Lieute-

nant Caldwell, commanding the sepoy escort, and Mr. Gordon, surgeon of the body-guard, who all accompanied me from Calcutta; and of Mr. Paton, Mr. Armstrong, Mr. Burney, and Mr. Shum, functionaries of this district who attended to render any assistance that might be required. Though we had not found game in anything like the quantity I expected, the party had been cheerful, and from the novelty of the scenes interesting. Its material advantage was, its giving me a view of a part of the country lying out of the course of ordinary expeditions up the river; a sort of sample by which one's notions of other tracts might be usefully regulated. In a military aspect, the whole which I have seen is a country for cavalry. Yet it is totally devoid of that arm. Indeed the paucity of provision in the hither provinces, an extent of territory which may be measured by four degrees of latitude and ten degrees of longitude, is altogether beyond belief. The incessant activity and the recognised equity of the Government can alone solve the problem how the enormous population of these districts is kept in tranquil obedience without any show of efficient strength.

February 21st.—Our boats had been ordered to meet us at Santipore, on the Hooghly, that we might have the advantage of a stronger current than we should have found in the Hurdum Nullah. Starting before daylight we rode half of the way, and then got into carriages which had been stationed to carry us the remaining eight miles. The villagers everywhere were ready with their little offerings. When within two miles of Santipore, I saw with anguish the sides of the road, which is a causeway devoid of trees, decorated with banana plants to make it look like an avenue. As each banana tree that is so cut is the loss of so much produce for the year, this sacrifice made by the poor people went to my heart. I had been acutely solicitous to prevent my excursions entailing inconvenience on any one. Where we encamped, every possible precaution was taken to hinder damage to any neighbouring field; and where injury could not be avoided, I made the collector assess the harm, and render compensation to the full satisfaction of the sufferer. The magistrate had been strictly enjoined by me to punish instantly and rigorously any person of the camp found guilty of petty oppressions on the inhabitants.   Three of my own suite having at an early period been seized and flogged for attempting little exactions, our police was most effectual, and here I saw the crop of hundreds of trees massacred without the possibility of my making good the loss.   The crowds of people that surrounded us were prodigious.   At length we reached the river.   Before I got into my boat, I was forced to have a kind of levee on the bank, that I might touch the nuzzurs of the principal natives.   There was much air of opulence and comfort among them.   Causing my thanks to be expressed to them for their attentions, I at last got into the boat.   The tide had just turned in our favour, and we went rapidly down the river. The distance, however, was too great to be achieved in one tide; and the flood having come against us, we were obliged to have the boats tracked down. It is surprising with what alacrity and cheerfulness the boatmen go through this heavy labour.   At five in the afternoon we reached Barrackpore; the poor fellows hailing it, as they approached, with a song.

June 23rd.—Notwithstanding the resolution I

had made of keeping my journal regularly, I have not been able to fulfil my intention. In truth, at Calcutta or Barrackpore, one's whole time is so invariably taken up with business that one is little in the way of observing chance occurrences. Then, all the particular features of public affairs are contained in the minutes I take, and cause to be copied into another book, of all that passes in Council worthy of notice; so that the entering them in this journal would be to make a duplicate record. Now that I am preparing to depart for the Upper Provinces it will be well to open the journal anew. By way of connexion, I have only to look back to the opinion with which I started respecting the natives. Every day more and more satisfies me that I formed a just estimate of those who inhabit Bengal at least. They are infantine in everything. Neat and dexterous in making any toy or ornament for which they have a pattern, they do not show a particle of invention; and their work unless they follow some European model, is flimsy and inadequate. Their religious processions constantly remind me of the imitation of some public ceremony which English children would make. One sees seven or eight persons gravely following a fellow who is tapping on a kind of drum that sounds like a cracked tin kettle, and though nobody looks at them they have the air of being persuaded that they are doing something wonderfully interesting. The temples they build are just such as would be constructed by schoolboys in Europe, had they the habit of dealing in brick and mortar. The edifices are rarely above four feet high, exclusive of two or three steps on which they are raised, and contain some rude and shabby carving or delineation of one or other of their gods. If this be the rate of the men, one may easily conceive what that of the women must be. Never enjoying even female society, their lives are passed in the extreme of listlessness. It is this which produces so many instances of women burning themselves. The husband's death is a revolution in their existence, which gives an opening for the mind's bursting out of the ordinary track of depression. They have a confused notion that the hour is the only one which can occur to them for distinction. As is the case with all spirits that have been long held in restraint, the momentary emancipation is carried to

extravagance. Working themselves up to frenzy
they pledge themselves to they know not what.
Once they declare their intention to burn themselves, which is done in the first instant of bewilderment produced by the husband's death, no retreat
is allowed. The forecasting policy of the Brahmins
has made the disgrace of the woman's faltering
fall, not on the individual alone, but on all her
relations, so that the whole of her family will force
her to perseverance. Then the Brahmins intoxicate
her with representations as well as with drugs. In
this hot climate the funeral of the defunct must so
soon take place that there is no time for reflection.
The interest of the Brahmins in this, is, that it is a
triumph over reason. The scene is an additional
perplexity to that common sense, the growth of
which they sedulously watch and endeavour to
stunt in the lower classes. Subjugation of the intellect, that they may reign over the bodies of the
multitude, is the unremitting object of that worth-
less and successful caste. One would imagine that
the habitual veneration which a Brahmin receives
from his earliest years was calculated to elevate his
mind and make him strive to appear worthy of his

high distinction by the dignified purity of his conduct. But this is so far from being the case, that in no class does one meet more frequent instances of vile and grovelling turpitude, as well as of deep atrocity. An example of the latter quality, recently reported by the judge of Benares, deserves insertion. A Brahmin had mortgaged a particular spot of land on terms which, according to the established law of the country, gave to the mortgagee the temporary cropping of the land. Having got the money, he would not surrender the land to the mortgagee, who sued him in Court and obtained an order to be put in possession. When the officer of the Court arrived at the field he found the Brahmin ploughing it, and required him to give it up. The Brahmin refused and assaulted the officer. In the scuffle, he got a slap in the face. There was no tolerating such an indignity, therefore the Brahmin went home and cut the throat of his eldest daughter, that her blood might be on the head of the person who had insulted him. The magistrate hearing of this act, sent to summon the Brahmin. This was a new affront; and by way of avenging it he killed his wife and his youngest daughter, persuading his brother to murder his daughter also for the honour of the family. The wretch, on being interrogated, avowed the murders without testifying the least degree of compunction.

June 24th.—This day I quitted Calcutta in form, having installed Sir G. Nugent as Vice-President. In strictness I cannot legally give him that title; but I wished to do it out of compliment, and it is only requisite that all acts of Council be confirmed by me.

We proceeded to Barrackpore, where the boats are to collect. It will take three days to assemble them.

June 26th—The hopes which I had expressed of having terminated matters amicably with the Nepaulese, have, unhappily, proved delusive Though nothing could be more clear than that they had trespassed beyond their known and established boundary, and had made most impudent encroachments upon our territory, the wish to settle matters without hostility, made us offer to submit the titles on both sides to commissioners. This was agreed to by the Rajah of Nepaul. The commissioners met. Those from Nepaul having not a shadow of pretension to substantiate against our irrefra-

gable proofs of right, went off suddenly.   Our
police and revenue officers were ordered to take
possession of the disputed tract.   They did so without opposition, and with the apparent acquiescence
of the latter.   The Nepaulese troops, however,
came down by night and surprised two of the
thannahs, murdering the police and revenue officers
with circumstances of extreme barbarity.   Since
that, they have attempted to poison the wells of
the villages on our frontier; not that we had any
troops there, but merely to destroy the innocent
ryots.   Great quantities of poison have been sent
from the interior of the country for that execrable
purpose, and a large body of archers with poisoned
arrows have reinforced the Nepaulese posts.   Having
a prodigious opinion of themselves from the con-
quests they have achieved, and knowing little of
our resources, they are now making a gallant
parade in our front.   They will pay for it by the
jungle fever which rages dreadfully in that district
during the rainy season.   The mortality heretofore
experienced by our sepoys from that cause will prevent my exposing any of our troops to the pesti-
lence at present.   When the cold season arrives,

the Nepaulese will be brought to account for this short triumph. In the meantime the Bettiah Provincial Battalion, accustomed to the climate, will sufficiently defend our frontier from incursions.

June 28th.—Embarked early in the morning; and our flotilla of something more than two hundred and twenty boats, weighed anchor instantly. We brought up in the afternoon off Hooghly. Mr. Brodie, judge of Hooghly, and Mr. Paton, judge of Kishnagur (whose district we enter to-morrow), came on board and dined with us. They brought their reports of the state of their districts. Our pinnace, the *Sonamuckhee*, is remarkably convenient, and sails very well. The children have another vessel equally good. The heat of the weather is excessive. It exceeded one hundred degrees of Fahrenheit in the cabins of the boats, in spite of all the mitigating precautions which luxury and experience have provided.

June 29th.—Got under weigh before sunrise. Our progress was not rapid, as we had very little breeze. Late in the afternoon we anchored about three miles short of the Santipore landing-place. The day was violently hot, but at night the air was somewhat cooled by a heavy fall of rain.   The temperature, however, was not lowered as much as one should have expected.

June 30th.—The little breath of air that existed being contrary, we made but slow progress in tacking up. The heat was intense. All the natives declare that they never had such hot weather before, and letters from Calcutta state that the heat is beyond what has been experienced there in any former year. Mr. Halhed, the assistant-judge of Burdwan, joined us to present his report of the state of his district, the judge (Mr. Bayley), being absent. The Rajah of Burdwan had prepared a curious salute for us on a sandy beach—a number of small mines which were exploded consecutively with plenty of noise. We anchored about half way between Santipore and Nuddeah.

July 1st.—Our progress was very slow. There was not a breath of air. The heat is greater than any man recollects it; therefore, the tracking of the boats against the stream was dreadfully fatiguing for the poor fellows. We anchored off Belpokareea, about three miles above Nuddeah. We had stopped so early that I landed my horses and got a ride. At a village some distance from the river, I saw several very large monkeys in a pepul tree. They paid no attention to the natives, but seemed agitated at finding themselves examined by the Europeans. Three of them were females carrying young in their arms; and the dexterity with which they managed their burthen while they were retreating to trees further from the road, was very interesting.

July 2nd.—Our progress was slow and uninteresting. We anchored about two miles short of Puttolee. After my horse was prepared, the appearance of a violent storm approaching, made me order it back again to its boat. The gust, however, when it arrived, proved to be without rain, though it brought clouds of dust with it. A short walk after the wind had subsided, was all the exercise manageable.

July 3rd.—Miserably slow progress. The stream was strong and not a breath of air. The heat violent. Just as we anchored, heavy rain came on and refreshed us much. There has been great sickness in the fleet, from the uncommon warmth of the weather.

July 4th.—The advance was little better than yesterday's, though we had two or three hours of stiff breeze. The excessive tortuousness of the channels did not allow us to make as much use of the wind as we had hoped. Fine showers came on in the afternoon; but there was a favourable pause, of which we profited, to get a ride after we had anchored. The eldest son of the Nawab, Dilwar Jung (of Calcutta), having come down from Moor-shadabad to pay his attentions, I received his visit.

July 5th.—Heavy rain in the morning. Great heat afterwards. The stream was strong, and wind unfavourable, so that we with difficulty got forward as far as Manickdee, where we anchored.

July 6th.—I got my horse very early, and rode to the field of Plassey; distant about four miles. One tree alone remains to mark where the tope stood; and, between the change which has taken place in the course of the river, and the obliteration of the entrenchments by the plough, no traces exist whence one can form a notion of the action. Anchored in the evening a little above Dondpoor. Mr. Leycester and Mr. Travers (collector), came down from Moorshadabad.

July 7th.—Rode along the banks of the river, and had the opportunity of observing how extraordinarily its course varies in the term of a few years. Anchored this evening a little above Jelalpoor.

July 8th.—Arrived off Berhampore about five o'clock, and were saluted by the field-pieces drawn up on the high bank, which prevents the river from overflowing the cantonment. Having received intimation that the garrison was under arms to receive me, I went ashore immediately; and having dismissed the troops to their barracks, had the officers presented to me. Mr. Brooke, agent of the Governor-General for the Nizamut, was waiting there to make arrangements with us. I fixed to dine and sleep at his house next day. Lady Loudoun came ashore, and we had a grand dinner at Major-General Morris's. He commands the station. He had prepared rooms for us; but we thought it more convenient to sleep aboard.

July 9th.—I reviewed in the morning the troops stationed at Berhampore, viz., his Majesty's 14th Foot, the Company's European Regiment, and a battalion of the 25th Native Infantry. They were in high order, and did their business perfectly well. We breakfasted with the officers of the 14th. Afterwards I had a levee, and gave audiences at Major-General Morris's.   In the evening, we drove to Mr. Brooke's, where we found much company assembled to meet us, and had an excellent dinner.

July 10th.—Rose very early that we might attend Divine service at Berhampore.   It was performed in a barrack, luckily vacant.   It is strange that when all the rest of the cantonment is on a scale absolutely magnificent, there should not be a place of worship there.   Visited the hospital, and found it in admirable order, though there were a number of patients still labouring under the Java fever.   After breakfast we went to see a collection of Hindoo antiquities and curiosities of the country, which has been formed with great activity and perseverance by Colonel Stuart.   The examination of it confirmed the opinion I had before entertained, that the present Hindoo mythology is not the depravation of a more rational system, but that from the beginning a wild incoherent and stupidly absurd pack of fancies were devised by the Brahmins to occupy the minds of the people.   Since their intercourse with us they have endeavoured to connect and reconcile their legends, in which they have had great assistance from the disposition of Europeans to find something abstrusely emblematical in the nonsense. There is not anything elegant in the remnants in Colonel Stuart's museum, either as to execution or as to taste. We gave a dinner afloat to the principal officers and ladies of the garrison.

July 11th.—Went very early to Mr. Brooke's, where the Nawab was to meet me at breakfast. Mr. Brooke's is five miles from Berhampore, and scarcely less from Moorshadabad. The country, though quite flat, is pretty. It is well wooded, and highly cultivated. The Nawab arrived about nine in barbaric state. The mixture of trappings, really handsome, with appendages ludicrously shabby, has a strange effect to our eyes, but never offends those of a native. After the Nawab's departure, I held a durbar for the principal native inhabitants of Moorshadabad. A number were presented to me. When this was finished I had long conversations on business with particular individuals. It was gratifying to me to find that

Lieutenant-General Palmer, whose ability and innate knowledge of Indian affairs render his opinion important, agreed with me perfectly as to the expedience (and indeed necessity) of extinguishing the fiction of the Mogul Government. This is also Mr. Brooke's earnest conviction from what he has seen in many years' management of the Nizamut affairs. With Mr. Brooke I had long discussions respecting the state of this and adjacent districts. His position gives him great insight, and he has not the inducements for colouring facts which may exist with the judicial officers and collectors. Major Paulby, who has the superintendence of the annual works for securing the city and its vicinity against inundations, gave me much interesting information. We dined with Mr. Brooke at four o'clock, and returned to sleep in our vessel.

July 12th.—Weighed anchor at dawn, for the purpose of breakfasting, according to engagement, with the Nawab. The wind was so unfavourable, and the tracking against the stream in a remarkably hot day so laborious, that we got on very slowly. The town of Cossimbazaar, from which the river has now considerably receded, may almost

be said to connect with Berhampore on one side,
and with Moorshadabad on the other, so as to form
a continuous population. The latter, though exceedingly extensive, has little the look of a city.
It consists of a number of villages clustered together with several small patches of tree-jungle
among them. The people, however, on the banks
were well dressed, and had an air of polish. It
was nearly mid-day before we got abreast of the
Nawab's palace, off which we anchored. A company of sepoys had been sent from Berhampore for
the occasion; and they, with the Grenadier company that formed my escort, occupied the ghaut or
landing-place. To gratify the Nawab, we consented
to be rowed ashore in a most splendid boat, which
he had just caused to be built. It was a mor-
punkha (peacock's feather) really elegant, but very
inconvenient. The howdah or seat, near the bows,
according to the fashion of those boats, was an extensive canopy of silver brocade, divided into three
domes, which were supported by silvered pillars.
The body of the boat was painted with flowers on
a yellow ground like a chintz. The effect was
equally light and rich, but the howdah afforded

little shelter from the sun. The boat must be from fourscore to ninety feet long. Her head and stern were so high out of the water, that the man who managed the oar with which she was steered, easily communicated (by dancing) a springing motion to those who sat in the howdah. Gaudy palankeens, belonging to the Nawab, were ready for us at the ghaut; but we preferred our own, and proceeded in them to the palace. The gateway was ruinous, and never could have been other than mean. The first and second courts within were neglected beyond conception: the buildings in a state of dilapidation, while weeds and rubbish filled the corners. The elephants, camels, cavalry, and sepoys were drawn up in these courts, and made a lively show. Passing through a narrow gorge, like an alley between two dead walls, we found ourselves on the sudden at the hall of the divan, on the entrance steps of which the Nawab was waiting to receive us. We embraced; after which he made his salaam to Lady Loudoun; and then offering each of us a hand, led us to the head of the breakfast table. The breakfast was mere matter of form, though handsomely laid out. The room was poor; the walls whitewashed;

arches ornamented with painted wood, coloured and carved with equal coarseness. A few English foxhunting prints, of the secondary rate, decorated one side. After a little while, some splendid jewels, with many trays of fine shawls and brocades, were offered. I took a common shawl handkerchief, which I said I would keep in remembrance of him, but declined the rest. Lady Loudoun took a muslin handkerchief, excusing herself from accepting any of the rich ornaments of pearl and emerald which she was pressed to receive. We then rose from table, and proceeded to visit the Walideh Begum, the Nawab going before to receive us at the zenana. We passed in our palankeens through some irregular ruinous courts, and even through the shambles where entrails and all kinds of filth were lying about. Arrived at an entrance which resembled the backway to some play-house, we got out of our palankeens and walked into the court round which the buildings are placed. There was not the least attempt at neatness in anything we saw. A few miserable shrubs only intimated that even the natural amusement of cultivating flowers was over-

looked.   The grand hall of audience, open to the
square, can be likened to nothing but the sort of
building one sees in the little tea-gardens about
London.   Half the building was separated from
the rest by sheets or coarse table-cloths sewed together.   Behind this sat the Begum.   Lady
Loudoun went within the curtain, where she found
everything correspondent to what met our eyes.
We talked through the screen.   When I desired
to take my leave, the Nawab (as he had done for
himself in his own apartments) desired permission
to put over my neck a wreath of foil.   It was gold,
silver, crimson, and green, so extraordinarily light
that great skill of workmanship must be required
to execute it.   They fall to pieces very readily, but
while they are fresh they are really pretty.   We
heard a violent contest behind the screen from the
Begum's insisting that Lady Loudoun should take
a splendid neoklace, which Lady Loudoun as
sturdily refused.   The Begum made many attempts
to throw it over Lady Loudoun's shoulders, and
resistance to this onset was the bustle we heard.   I
was forced to interfere, and I requested Mr. Brooke
to explain the invincible resolution Lady Loudoun

had taken of not accepting any present of intrinsic value while she should be in India; a determination which we could not hope these people should comprehend, but to which they were forced to bow. Lady Loudoun represents the Walideh Begum as vulgar in appearance and manners. We thence went to the Douleen Begum, the favourite wife of the Nawab. She was better lodged than the Walideh; still, all looked patched and incongruous. Our ceremony here was similar to what we had before experienced. The curtain was of rather better materials, yet only striped stuff and dirty. Magnificent jewels were urgently pressed on Lady Loudoun, and refused. She only took a little bottle of sandal-wood oil. We then proceeded to the Bhow Begum, the Nawab's other wife, where exactly the same forms took place. I was surprised at the insolent authority with which the head eunuch (who was on our side of the curtain) spoke to the poor woman. She probably had not understood something which Mr. Brooke said to her on my part, on which the eunuch in a high voice and tone of reprehension asked her why she did not answer. Remarking this to the gentleman next to

me, who happened to be long conversant with the
manners of the country, I was told these fellows
were allowed to treat the women with great harsh-
ness. We here took leave of the Nawab, and returned to our vessel strongly impressed with the
shabbiness and misery of an Asiatic zenana. There
were within the walls of the palace very many
beggars who harassed us with uncommon impor-
tunity.

At eight at night we repaired to the Roshen
Baugh, a palace or villa which the Nawab has built
for himself, on the west side of the river. It
is simply a gentleman's house, distinguished by
nothing of furniture, except that at each end of the
two principal rooms there were handsome mirrors.
We were led by the Nawab, who met us on the
steps, to a verandah behind the house, whence we
saw a kind of transparent wall, fashioned in a
variety of colours, which had a good effect. A
nautch commenced as soon as we seated ourselves
on the sofa. Here I was again struck with the in-
consistency which appears in all the arrangements
of these people. Fond as they are of the nautch,
the effect of this part of the entertainment was

destroyed by two rows of men who stood the whole length of the room, in the centre, with large embroidered hand-punkhas to fan the guests on each side. The play of these punkhas allowed one to eatch only momentarily the gestures of the performers. The strain of the song was in general monotonous: and it seemed as if amidst all the modulations the great effort was to make the sound of the English *a* in father predominant with a marked nasal tone. Fireworks, very good, were now let off. Then we were summoned to supper. It was handsome; in the English, or rather in the Anglo-Indian style, with loads of meat and variety of wines. There were decorations of artificial fruit, in wax, admirably executed. After supper we took leave of the Nawab, and returned to our boats.

July 13th.—Weighed anchor at day-break. A fresh breeze rose and carried us forward rapidly. Sometimes the squalls were fresh, and a boat was overset. The crew were all saved. The cargo was only charcoal for the supply of my cooking boat. We anchored in the evening off Nasipore.

July 14th.—The wind being fair and fresh we arrived at an early hour off Jungpore, where we had promised to stop and dine with Mr. Ramsay. We examined the winding of his silk. The moths are four times the size of those in Italy, and quite a different kind. The cocoons are small: three of them, I should imagine, would not contain as much silk as one of the Italian. We had an excellent dinner, and slept on board.

July 15th.—Reached the cut between the Banghretty and the Ganges, near Sooty, early in the afternoon, but as the current was so strong against us, with an unfavourable wind, as to make it clear that the getting through would be a long operation for the fleet, we brought-to for the night. I walked to the cut to examine it. There had been in this place a small channel, which, when the waters were very high, afforded a temporary and occasional communication with the Ganges. The obstruction to navigation experienced for some months every year, on account of the shoals at the natural junction of the Banghretty with the Ganges, induced our Government to try whether by making a canal (in the direction indicated by the course of the flood) across a narrow sandy strip, a permanent communication might not be effected.

The cut was accordingly undertaken. As soon as the water of the river was led into it the force of the stream achieved what was far beyond expectation. It has ploughed a channel of considerable depth, about one hundred and fifty yards in breadth; and the flow of water through it is such as gives every reason to believe that the junction is secure for every season.

July 16th.—By day-break we attempted the passage. It was a laborious undertaking, each boat being to be haled through by large gangs from the neighbouring villages, added to their own crews. As soon as each got into the Ganges it could set its sails to a fresh of wind. Of course sad distance between the vessels would have been occasioned had we not merely slanted up for a little way, and then anchored near the further shore. No village designated the place, but it was in a line with the ruins of Gour. As we passed through the cut, great masses of the elevated bank fell into the water. The force of the stream is rapidly undermining the southern shore, and I should not be surprised were the Hooghly to become, in consequence, a still more considerable branch of the

Ganges than it now is. The original course of the Banghretty into the Ganges, near Mohungunge, is likely to become impassable, except in the height of the floods.

July 17th.—Sunday.—We proceeded no further than to Seebgunge, where we waited to let our flotilla collect. The boats had suffered great difficulties from the strength of the current and violence of the gusts. Two boats, with sepoys of the escort, ran foul of each other, and both had a side stove in. The men were got out into other boats before their vessel sank. We had divine service in the evening.

July 18th.—Had a fine breeze, and anchored in the evening off Furruckur, erroneously called Furrackabad in Reynell's map.

July 19th.—With a favourable wind we reached Rajemahl by mid-day. In the evening I rode about two miles into the country, to see the ancient palace of the Soubahdars of Bengal. It is all in ruins, and can never have been worthy of notice. It has no extent for magnificence, and the small remains of tracery work give no reason to think there was any nicety or elegance of ornament belonging to it. Its name of Phul-Baugh, indicating a place where flowers were cultivated, makes it probable that this was considered as a retired villa, though there is nothing in the spot to recommend the building a retreat there.

July 20th.—Went in the morning to see the remains of the palace on the bank of the river. It has been on a considerably larger scale than the other, yet there is little to persuade one that it could ever have been splendid. The marble hall is the principal object to which the natives call your attention. The room is only 21 feet long by 15 broad. It is floored with black marble, slightly, and not inelegantly, inlaid with white. The walls are of a coarse white marble. Nothing of the ornaments commands any attention, except some sentences in the Persian character, inlaid with black marble in the white, round one of the doors. The arches have much of the Gothic turn. No impression of magnificence was left by these ruins.

July 24th.—While the fleet was preparing to sail I got a ride on the plain. I remarked many of the nests of the white ants of extraordinary height. One of them could not be under ten feet, as it was a great deal higher than my head, though the horse I was riding was very tall. These nests are conical, and appear too thin to stand against the weather; yet they resist the rains and storms perfectly. Several of them were clothed with a leafy creeper like bindweed, quite to the top, and had a singular appearance. About the middle of the day it began to blow fresh, with heavy showers of rain. The tide which we were stemming was very rapid; and three crazy vessels, unable to bear the strain, foundered; but their crews were luckily saved. The passage close to Vidhya Soornag (the Holy Cave) is dangerous on account of the rocks and the violence of the current; so that, as we had a favourable breeze for getting through it, I did not land to examine some antiquities which are to be seen at the spot. The place is in Reynell's map erroneously called Pointye, which is the name of a village at a little distance inland. I have seen drawings of these antiquities, which are basso-relievos on a small scale cut in the rock. They exhibit the Indian divinities, with this only re-markable, that the faces have the features of the hill people; namely, broad nostrils and thick lips, though not of the negro character. After some misadventures from vessels running foul of each other through the whirls of the current, we anchored a little short of Colgong, and had divine service.

July 25th.—I rode in the morning to a house, belonging to a Mr. Davidson, which has a complete view of the rocks of Colgong, as well as of the inland country. The latter is wild and picturesque; being chiefly scattered wood upon knolls which are the spurs of the Rajemahl Hills. The rocks are also striking. There are two of them. They appear like mounds of vast stones which had originally been soft, and rounded by the current. Some huts are built on each, and there are a few trees growing out of the fissures. The current is exceedingly strong between these rocks and the shore; so that the vessels are forced to be tracked through it; and there is the risk of the guy-rope's breaking, in which case the boat could not fail to be thrown on the rocks. We reached Baughlipore (quitting the main river and going up a nullah) in the afternoon. Sir Frederick Hamilton, the collector, had met us down the river, and was now to

be our host.   Before we went to his house we took
our evening's airing.   Lady Loudoun and I went
on an elephant, and the rest of the party in carriages, to see the house built by Mr. Cleveland and
his monument.   The house is finely situated on a
hill commanding an extensive view of the Ganges
and adjacent country.   They assured us here that
at certain times the Nepaul hills can be seen from
the upper part of this house, though the reputed
distance be 200 miles.   They say that this only
happens when there has been a considerable fall of
rain for some hours, rendering the atmosphere
peculiarly clear.   The monument aims not at elegance.   In truth, though the elevation of it was a
proper and politic recognition of the individual's
merits by the Company, the erection of it was in
other respects superfluous.   The reverence which
at an early age Mr. Cleveland had created for himself in the minds of the natives will not suffer his
name to sink into oblivion.   The natives reared a
monument to him at the other end of the town.
It contains a small chamber into which they often
go to pray; and in the lapse of a century or two
the name of Cleveland is likely to be confounded

with manifold appellations which they have for each of their divinities. We dined and slept at Sir Frederick's, where the hospitality was in the best tone.

July 26th.—Rode out early in the morning. The extent and population of the town is greater than I had imagined. A Mahommedan mosque there is in a better style of building, and more elegantly ornamented as to the friezes, than anything I have before seen in this country. Some of the tracery was worthy of introduction into England, and we had it copied. In the evening we went to see an indigo work. The arrangements are coarse though expensive. From what I recollect of indigo works in Carolina, I should think much improvement might be made here. We then proceeded to look at some remnants of antiquity which Major Franklin had collected. There was not anything striking either in conception or execution. In the course of the day I saw a curious exhibition. It was a bear who went through all the forms of a Hindostanee wrestling-match with his keeper. The creature seemed to understand the trick perfectly, and preserved its good temper while its master rolled over and over with it on the ground. It was not muzzled.

July 27th.—Having taken leave of our hosts overnight, we rose at three that I might review the corps of Hill Rangers about five miles from Baughlipore, our vessels being directed to proceed along the nullah parallel to our road. The corps, composed of men from the Rajemahl Hills, went through its business extraordinarily well. The Commandant, Major Littlejohn, detaches parties in succession to shoot game with their muskets in the hills; a practice admirable for rendering the men expert with their pieces, as well as ready at getting through the tangled woods with which all hilly ground in India is covered.

After the review, we went to see two insulated towers in the neighbourhood. They have some resemblance to the round towers in Ireland; but are not above half the height to which those have been ordinarily raised. The door in these Indian towers is on a level with the ground : whereas, in all the towers I have seen in Ireland the door is at an elevation not to be reached but by a ladder. Evidently, those which I saw this day were of no considerable antiquity. Some Brahmins, by appointment, brought to us a stone with an inscription of extraordinary age. There seems to be no contest among the learned in Hindoo lore as to admitting the inscription to bear a date about 600 years before Christ; but a term far anterior is insisted upon for it by many. It is lucky that it is now in the hands of the Brahmins, who never let it see the day but on grand occasions, as the presents they receive when they do produce it gives them an interest to preserve it from accident.

Having reached our boats we soon got out of the nullah into the river, along the bank of which we were forced to track. This gave an opportunity to a number of men and women, all apparently in perfect health and able to work, to harass us with begging. The style is peculiarly revolting, as it really is an attempt to wear you into submission by clamour. We had undergone the same at Baughlipore and at the review ground. A breeze springing up, we hoisted sail, and passed Jangheera, a temple to Sheeva, built on one of two rocks, which rise nearly in the mid-stream of the river. The current here ran with such rapidity that many of our vessels could not stem it, and were thrown sadly astern. We were forced, that the separation might not become still greater, to anchor for the night on the north side of the river, about half way between Baughlipore and Monghyr. The Corruckpore hills furnished a fine termination to the view in one direction.

July 28th.—Adverse wind, and the strength of the current allowed us to make but little progress, and the fleet got entangled amid sand banks, which occasioned great separation. We brought-to about seven miles short of Monghyr, to let the other vessels rejoin us. This day and yesterday we have seen a number of persons floating down the stream by means of an empty earthenware jar (well corked) under each arm. Nearer to Baughlipore, some of them carried milk-pots on their heads for sale at that place. This mode of voyaging has little of trouble in it, for it requires no exertion; but there is great peril from the alligators. That danger is solved to each individual by his belief that if it be his fate to be devoured by an alligator, the creature would come and take him out of his bed.

July 29th.—The wind was still unfavourable,

and the river very rough. Three vessels which had struck against each other, went down; but only two men were lost. In the afternoon we anchored at Sittacoon. We went ashore to see the hot spring. It rises in the plain in the middle of a small brick tank which has been made around it. The spring is by no means copious. It raised Fahrenheit's thermometer to 145°. I was told that two months hence the temperature will be much lower. This of course must arise from the draining of the water during the rainy season into those cavities in which the steam from still more profound reservoirs is condensed before it visits the surface. The water is pure and tasteless. Having satisfied our curiosity at the spring, we went to see a house built by General Ellerker, on the Peer Puhur, an elevated rocky hill. The prospect is extraordinarily extensive and singularly varied. On the other side of the river vast plains stretch themselves to the north. The hither view consisted of a number of craggy monticules in a flat which reached to the Corruckpore hills. These monticules strikingly display what has been the operation of nature in that spot. The same subterranean fire which heats the water has, by causing air to expand in cavities below, forced up the strata of clay so as to throw them on their edges at the centre of each hill; baking at the same time the mass into a kind of coarse slaty stone. I could not perceive any fragments whence one could infer the explosion of fire at the surface.

July 30th.—Proceeded in carriages to Monghyr, while our boats were to advance along the shore. The remains of the fort present little remarkable. It is of such extent that it immediately suggests the solution of the facility with which so many of the Indian forts have been carried by escalade. The guarding properly such a length of rampart, would require a prodigious garrison, even were the troops of the best disciplined and most alert description. The works have been suffered to go entirely to decay, the altered circumstances of our dominion no longer attaching any interest to this particular position. Yet the rampart ought to be prevented from falling; because the case might occur in which a refuge of this nature, whither the neighbours might carry valuable property, were the country overrun by hostile cavalry, would be

very useful. I examined specimens of various manu-
factures here. The natives have imitated British
fowling-pieces and rifles with great skill. These
fire-arms are very neatly made; but the barrels are
apt to burst. The articles which I saw did great
credit to the ingenuity of the workmen. There is
much alarm here about the state of the crops in a
wide tract around this place. They have not had
a drop of rain since the 17th of last month, though
this is the wet season.

July 31st.—We had divine service at seven in
the morning, on board our boat. Some officers
and ladies from the station attended. The wind
was unfavourable; therefore a trial was made
whether vessels could be tracked past the fort, for
which purpose measures had been taken the evening before. The stream sets with violence against
a rock on which a bastion of the fort is built.
Two smaller boats were warped past the bastion
with some difficulty. The third, of larger size, was
whirled against the rock, and went down immediately. No life was lost; but all that belonged
to the detachment of sepoys embarked in the boat
was either carried away or ruined. Towards the

afternoon, heavy rain came on, and continued through the night, but without changing the wind. The superstition of the natives gave me credit for the salutary showers.

August 1st.—The wind being still against us, I rode out in the morning. The vicinage of Monghyr is thickly studded with villages. I went through some of them. It struck me as very remarkable, that human creatures living for so great a length of time in rather a civilized state of society, should not have attained a better notion of daily practical convenience. They seem to have been totally insensible to the fact that a straight line from one place to another is the shortest; and the wretched serpentine paths which lead one through their villages must be a constant embarrassment to them in driving their cattle, sheep, and goats, out to pasture.

The Irish peasant makes shifts from want of means, the Bengalee from choice with superabundance of materials at his disposal. Nor is it indolence that withholds the latter, for the poor fellows show much exertion when they wish to effect anything. The news that the allies had entered Paris reached us this morning. It came by way of Constantinople to Bombay. The rain came on again extraordinarily heavy, so that one may now trust the crops are secure. It continued raining all the evening.

August 2nd.—The fleet remained wind-bound; the day rainy. Some persons floating down the middle of the stream on kedgeree (earthenware) pots, with small umbrellas over their heads, presented a singular appearance. Mr. Mackenzie, Mr. Sealy, and Mr. Blagrove, who had come to pay their official attendance, joined us this day.

August 3rd.—Continuation of the foul wind, with very heavy rain. An attempt was made to tow or track one of our vessels round the bastion; but the two ropes broke through the violence of the stream, and the vessel had a narrow escape from perishing. Between the showers the heat (as it was the two former days) has been excessive.

August 4th.—Still detained; with the same weather, and no occurrence.

August 5th.—We took advantage of a slight shift of wind to make a slant across the river, in hopes of thence clearing the bastion, by going on the other tack. The wind failed us as we reached the opposite shore, where we anchored just below some very dangerous rocks. In the evening a breeze arose, and we hoisted sail. The wind being but faint, and the current excessively strong, the few vessels which were with us but just cleared the bastion, and drifted into a kind of bay behind it. This pass of Monghyr is a seriously embarrassing one. Boats have often been detained at it for three weeks. The fleet was much separated, because the greater part of the vessels which had attempted to cross the river with us in the morning had been caught in the middle of the stream by the calm, and had been carried down a long way.

August 6th.—A favourable wind and very fresh, arose in the night. It soon brought up to us the distant vessels, so that about nine in the morning we also made sail. We ran along a shore displaying the remains of many mosques and tombs, indicating the former grandeur of Monghyr. When I say splendour, I mean it in the Indian sense; for it is impossible to look at the remains of any of these cities which have been the residences of Moslem or Hindoo sovereigns, and not to be struck with one particular deficiency. There is scarcely in the neighbourhood of any of these places the vestige of a regular road. Yet, in the vicinity of Monghyr there is plenty of stone for the formation of so great and obvious a convenience. I do not forget the road at Kishnagur. But there was in that more notion of magnificence in planting an avenue of vast extent, than of commodity for the public as to communication. We ran with a fair wind about twenty miles, and anchored off the village of Soorajigunuh.

August 7th.—The chaplain's boat having broke the tow-rope, was carried so far away by the stream that he could not reach us to perform divine service during the course of the day.

After having delayed our progress above three hours in expectation of him, we made sail and advanced about fourteen or fifteen miles. We brought-to in a narrow branch of the river, with a rich and highly cultivated country on each side. I was told that from these grounds the farmers uniformly got three crops in the year, never manuring the land, or letting it lie fallow. The river at times overflows it, and deposits so much mud as sufficiently recruits the soil. If a tumbler-full of water be now taken from the Ganges, the earth which speedily subsides from it will occupy nearly a fourth part of the glass.

August 8th.—Slow progress and excessive heat. Anchored not far from Derriapore.   The country rich and highly cultivated.

August 9th.—Our advance has been still slow, from want of wind, and from great heat, which oppress the men who track the boats.   We passed Bar, a populous town, and brought-to for the night close to a village on an island.

August 10th.—My ride this morning was rendered disagreeable, as it has been for the last two days, by the hollowness of the ground, which the rats have undermined in a strange manner.   The rats are about the size of a full grown guinea-pig, and are pied yellow and white.   The heat and great strength of the stream delayed our progress, and we anchored ten miles short of the custom-house of Patna.   Mr. Money, the collector, joined the fleet yesterday.

August 11th.—Though our distance was so short, the stream was so strong that we did not anchor off Bankipore (the further part of Patna) till after dark.   This was not for want of wind.   We literally, after passing the custom-house, scarcely made way ahead with a gust which overset three vessels. We landed and took up our quarters in the house of Mr. Duncan Campbell, who superintends the package of the opium here for the Company.

August 12th.—An address was presented to me by the Europeans resident at Patna.

As soon as the sun was near setting I rode out, but I got encircled by such a crowd, which accompanied me throughout the ride, that I might rather be said to take the steam than take the air. The people were very respectful, for which the inhabitants of Patna are not famous. The population consists very much of Moguls; and as the better families of them are barred from most of the advantageous lines of life by the system of our government, they are very apt to sow dissatisfaction among the lower classes. This being the Prince Regent's birthday, in honour of him, as well as on occasion of the recent news from Europe (the suppression of Napoleon and limitation of France to reasonable boundaries), I ordered the enlargement of eighteen convicts under sentence of perpetual labour in chains. We had at night a splendid entertainment given by Mr. Campbell to the European ladies and gentlemen.

August 13th.—Rode in the morning to see the Golah.

This is a brick building, rising as a dome, constructed by order of Mr. Hastings, as one of many receptacles for grain which he meditated establishing, with the view of guarding against famine. This building seems admirably calculated for the purpose. Its height, and its diameter, are about 100 feet. The wall is very thick and well built. Four doors, on a level with the ground, afforded facility for taking out the grain. Two spiral staircases lead by an easy ascent to the top, where the grain was to be delivered into the building by a central aperture. The plan was that in cheap years rice should be purchased and accumulated in buildings of that sort, till each should be full. No second Golah has been built, and no grain has ever been lodged in this one. I understand it is urged that grain would swell and spoil if laid up in such a mass, and that the having such a resource (if the grain did not spoil) would make the people less active in tilling the ground. I am not satisfied of the validity of these objections. The supposition that the grain would spoil is gratuitous. Rice in the husk, if kept secure from the weather, will remain good for very many years, and inattention to the cultivation of the lands is by no means a consequence that can be connected with such a provision. The horrors of the famine, which stimulated Mr. Hastings to undertake this magnificent system of securing the natives from the recurrence of so dreadful a calamity, appear to have been too soon forgotten. Unquestionably, there is now much more soil in culture than there was at that time; but peculiarities of season may defeat all the confidence which rests on that circumstance; and this very year the delay of rain for ten days more would probably have ruined all the expectant crops. The alarm was very great.

The cultivation of potatoes is spreading fast, and will be a material security against dearth; but it does not yet go to an extent to be reckoned upon. In the middle of the day I held a durbar.

Two brothers of the late Saadut Aly presented their nuzzurs, as did likewise all the principal natives residing at Patna. I gratified, in a peculiar degree, Gundshaum Singh by granting permission for his wearing at the durbar (which without such leave would have been inadmissible) a sabre, bestowed upon him by Lord Wellesley for the activity of his service with Lord Lake.

He presented his nuzzur on the flat of the blade. I touched both the mohurs and the sword, when he kissed the latter, and swore by it that he would be ready to obey my call, with as many men as he could influence, whensoever I might summon him to the field.   He is a fine sturdy looking fellow. As soon as he got out of the room he cried in recounting to those around him the kindness with which I had spoken to him.   Our people are much too negligent of those little winning attentions which operate strongly on the feelings of the natives.   We think that the simplicity of our address and habits must be comprehended by them.   But in fact they are too prone to ascribe those manners in us to our holding the natives too cheap to care what they may think with regard to us.

After a durbar which I held at Calcutta, a rajah said to the public secretary "This man knows what " to say to us.   You ought always to have a great

" sirdar at the head of the government. ———

" ——— was of the weaver cast, and he could

" not flatter us with anything he said!"   I this day bestowed khilauts on the Maharajah Muttree Jeet Singh and the Maharajah of Tirhoot. The latter is of the older family, but I gave a precedence to the other on account of his personal character. I desired him to understand that my investing him with the dress of honour was not merely for his attachment to the British Government, but proceeded from my knowledge that he had made all the ryots under him comfortable and happy, a tenor of conduct which I wished to distinguish by that public applause. After the durbar, a dwarf was produced. He was seventeen years of age; about the ordinary height of a child five years old, but of lighter make. His head was small, and his countenance good. There was nothing of that want of proportion which usually characterises dwarfs.

We went in the evening to see the opium warehouse, where it is collected from the neighbouring districts, and packed in chests for transmission to Calcutta.

The building is curious. It is of brick, and of great solidity. I could not learn by whom it had been built. The plan is said to have been furnished by an Italian to one of the native princes, but this tradition appeared very vague. I could get no better satisfaction as to its original purpose. At each corner of a square centre, rising higher than the rest of the building, is a staircase (of brick), placed on segments of arches. From the flat terrace top an extensive view of the city is commanded. The town is long and narrow. Its population is estimated at above 200,000. It has more the air of a city than anything which I have before seen in India. The part of Calcutta, in the vicinity of the Government House, is splendid. But the remainder of the city consists of huts composed chiefly with mats and thatch. Here almost all the houses are substantial. The richer natives have good brick houses. The mansions of the lower classes are principally mud-walled (the *pisé* of France) with good tiled roofs. Immense crowds followed us, testifying respect and satisfaction. We dined with Mr. Welland, first Judge of the Provincial Court of Circuit.

August 14th.—We had divine service at Mr. Campbell's.   It was numerously attended.   At sunset or a little earlier I went out to ride.   The streets were thronged with people waiting for our coming out.   Nothing could be more reverential than their behaviour; which I mention for the purpose of remarking how practically essential it is a public functionary should keep up a degree of state, such as may operate on the eyes of the multitude.   This unusual tone of the populace has been noticed by all the English gentlemen here, yet they do not seem to reason from it.   At some little distance from the town I perceived a collection of people; on approaching I found it was Gundshaum Singh with a numerous tribe of attendants. He had stationed himself there that he might have a chance of seeing me.   He ran forward with a joyful eagerness, which was really touching, and entreated me to lay my hand on his sword.   When I had done so, speaking cordially to him, he reiterated his oath of attending me with his followers wheresoever I might require his service.   As he is opulent and liberal, he has many adherents.

At dinner I tasted some wine which Mr. Havel

sent to me for trial. He is a person who has made a large fortune by supplying the navy and army with provisions. The wine was but three months old, and this is the first attempt at making wine in these parts; the result is very encouraging. The present wine is likely to become very agreeable when the sweetness is somewhat gone off. But it is probable that experience will teach the art of making wine of a still higher quality. Grapes are said to thrive extraordinarily well in this district. We have had many figs, but they are devoid of flavour.

August 15th.—The repair of damages sustained by our fleet prevented our departure. Nothing particular occurred. In the evening Lady Loudoun went to see a Sikh temple. The gentlemen who accompanied her said that there could not be less than 50,000 persons collected round it, as her intended visit was known.

They were struck, as they had been on former occasions, with the marked deference of the crowd. I experienced exactly the same tone in the quarter in which I had ridden.

August 16th.—Our boats having preceded us

yesterday evening, we went in carriages to Dinapore (eight miles), where I reviewed a battalion of the 13th Native Infantry. They were in good order. The cantonment here, containing barracks for a strong regiment of European infantry, is a fine establishment. The country around it is in the highest state of cultivation, and a great air of opulence marks the whole neighbourhood. A public breakfast was given by Major-General Marley at Mr. Havel's house. It stands in the midst of a farmyard on a most extensive scale, admirably laid out, and kept in the neatest condition.

After breakfast we embarked; but for want of wind we were not able to proceed above four miles. The part of the river where we were was very unfavourable for tracking.

August 17th.—We attempted to get forward at daybreak, but a dead calm, with excessive heat, soon forced us to stop.

Many of the boats were carried a long way down by the stream. After midday excessively heavy rain came on, and lasted about two hours. It was followed by a fine breeze, of which the whole fleet took advantage. It suddenly began to blow fresh. And a vessel with baggage was over-set owing to the incorrigible habit of the boatmen to tie the sheets of their sails in such a manner as that they never can suddenly be let fly. We did not make ten miles in the course of the day. Mr. Younge and Mr. Mitford, the acting judge and acting collector of Sarun had joined us; as had also Mr. Vaughan, the judge of Sha-habad.

August 18th.—We got as far as Chuprah, where we anchored. It is the principal town of the zillah, but resembles a long straggling village. The case of a lad of seventeen, under capital sentence here for child-murder, led to shocking information about the prevalence of that crime in this vicinity. The deliberate premeditated murder of a poor infant for the sake of stealing its little ornaments, worth but a few shillings at most, is an atrocity which, without such proof, one could not have conceived frequent in any state of society. An instance was detailed to me where a woman cut the throat of her own nephew, a fine boy be-tween five and six years old, in order to appropriate to herself his bangles, the value of which she must have accurately known.   They were worth, in English money, one shilling and tenpence half-penny.   These effects, in the absence of inculcated morals, in a people of placid temper, afford much ground for reflection.

August 19th.—Reached Buxar. The strength of the wind opposed to the current made the water exceedingly rough.   Since we have got above the confluence of the Dewah and Gogra, the breadth of the river has diminished much.   It is not here a mile and a half wide, but it is deep. Colonel Toone (the commandant), and the rest of the station staff, came off to me.   I went ashore with him to look at the fort.   It is small, with four round bastions.   The ditch is wide, and the brick revetement of the works is in good order.   No neighbouring ground commands it.   Going to the edge of the cliff on which the fort stands, in order to look at the reach of the river, I saw a boat over-set by a sudden gust.   Her crew, eight men and a boy, clung to the rigging, but were carried down the stream, and whirled in the eddies with great rapidity.   Not a boat, of the many sailing near them, attempted to give them any succour.   My own boat did not push off from the beach till after repeated calls from me, and then proceeded with a languor quite disgusting. The insensibility of the natives towards each other is astonishing. All the poor fellows belonging to the wrecked boat were saved.

August 20th.—Sailed from Buxar. Heavy storms of rain came on; and, the smaller boats not being able to face the gusts, we lost the best part of the day under the shelter of the northern bank. In the afternoon we passed the mouth of the Carumnassa. The disposition of the Hindoos seems peculiarly turned to venerate rivers; yet against this particular stream there exists a prejudice which I have not heard well explained. A Hindoo who shall have to ferry over this river, when on a pilgrimage to any of the sacred places, suffers indescribable anxiety, lest any splash from the oars should touch his garments. If a single drop of the water of the Carumnassa rest upon him, all his past labour goes for nought; and he must begin his pilgrimage anew, or pay a grievous sum to the Brahmins for his purification. We stopped for the night near the village of Sairpoor.

August 21st.—We arrived in the afternoon off Ghazypore. Colonel Hardyman, commanding the King's 17th Foot and the station, came aboard. At five I went ashore, and walked to the monument of Lord Cornwallis. It was painful to see it unfinished, so long after his death. But as Government, just before I left Calcutta, allotted money for completing it with all despatch, it will not remain in this disgraceful state. The freestone with which it is constructed comes from Chunar, and is of excellent quality. This being Sunday, we had divine service in a tent ashore. Mr. Brooke, governor-general's agent at Benares; Mr. Craycroft, register; and Mr. Harding, acting commercial resident, came to me.

August 22nd.—I received aboard the *Sonamukhee* the Rajah of Benares, who had come to present his nuzzur. He is prodigiously large and fat, but with a lively and good countenance. I had previously (at daybreak) reviewed the 17th regiment. He was *incognito* on the field, and was much struck with the performance of the troops; they were in high order. After the review we breakfasted with the officers of the corps.

Ensign Stephens, acting engineer at Benares, came to me there. As soon as the Rajah's visit was over we weighed anchor. We proceeded little more than six miles; but we had not expected to make much progress, and our object was to get out of the bight of Ghazypore, lest an unfavourable wind should catch us in it. The river at Ghazypore is narrowed to about half a mile; of course it is very deep, and the current prodigious. It sometimes runs at the rate of eight knots an hour.

August 23rd.—We had a leading breeze, very fresh, and made great way. At Chochuckpore there is a fine ghaut, or flight of stairs, of freestone, and of great breadth. A temple stands near the top of it. One of our attendants, who was walking along the bank, saw a number of monkeys on a large banian tree. He opened his bag, and offered them some bread; on which they descended and picked up the pieces round his feet, without any seeming apprehension. They are never molested in the neighbourhood of the temples. Mr. Wilberforce Bird, magistrate of the city of Benares, and Mr. Salmon, collector, joined us. We are to reside at the house of the latter; therefore I emancipated him immediately that he might be ready to receive us.

August 24th.—For the last two or three days the heat has been very great. This day it became quite oppressive; the thermometer was at 98°. Of course the tracking (what little breeze there was being unfavourable) was too laborious for us to make much progress. At night violent rain, with heavy gusts and much lightning, came on; yet the air was scarcely cooled. During the day, what is emphatically called the hot wind had reigned. I was made to observe that drinking-glasses, which stood perfectly sheltered from the sun, had become quite warm from the temperature of the atmosphere. Lieutenant Morrieson, station engineer of Chunar, joined the fleet.

August 25th.—I indulged myself in a good walk along the bank, while the boats were tracking tediously. Since I left Calcutta, I have seldom missed getting a ride either morning or evening; yet, although I have on these occasions usually deserted the beaten path, and have gone to some distance in the deserted fields, I have not seen a single snake. This proves that they cannot be numerous; of course, danger from them is little to be apprehended. We anchored within a mile and a half of Raj Ghaut, the eastern extremity of Benares, between eight and nine at night, too late to think of landing.

August 26th.—Landed at six o'clock at Raj Ghaut, where I found Mr. Brooke, Mr. Salmon, Mr. Bird, and other gentlemen waiting for me. Proceeded to Mr. Salmon's house, where, in the middle of the day, I had a levee. The civilians who attended it were Mr. Brooke, Mr. Sanford, Mr. Courtney Smith, Mr. Rattray, Mr. Brown, Mr. Wilberforce Bird, Mr. Bird, jun., Mr. Harding, Mr. Harding, jun., Mr. Forde, Mr. Boldero, Mr. Lindesay, Mr. Wynne, Rev. Mr. Brodie, Dr. Yeld, and Mr. Robinson. Major Wilford was also present. Lady Loudoun did not land till the evening, having been somewhat indisposed.

August 27th.—I had risen before day to ride, but such heavy rain came on as obliged me to remain at home. I therefore betook myself to papers, and continued working at them from that early hour with only the interval of breakfast and of audiences till evening. I found myself uncommonly exhausted; but as Mr. Salmon gave a great entertainment to the gentlemen of the station, I was obliged to attend at dinner. My efforts, however, to resist the weight of fatigue were fruitless, for at length I fainted. On recovering, I was sensible of much feverish feel, and readily connected this debility with a restlessness which had prevented my getting sleep for two preceding nights.

August 28th.—I remained confined with considerable fever. My indisposition obliged me to put off receiving the visit which the princes, brothers of the King of Delhi, were to pay me this day. Last night the whole city of Benares was brilliantly illuminated out of compliment to me. The attention is the more particular, because that the inhabitants are a very turbulent set, and in general undisguised contemners of Government. As all the English gentlemen live at Secrole, between four and five miles from Benares, no example of theirs could influence this procedure. Mr. Brooke was desired by me to express this day my acknowledgments to some of the leading natives. They laughed, and said, " You think us hot-headed, troublesome fellows, but we have our own notions of propriety, and follow them."

August 29th.—I remained confined, and interdicted from attending to business.

August 30th.—Though by no means recovered, I did not like to put off the princes again; therefore I received them at twelve o'clock. They were as follows:—Mirza Khoorrum Bukht, son of Jehandar Shah, eldest son of Shah Aalum. Jehandar Shah having died in the lifetime of his father, by the Mahomedan law the right of succession passed away from his children to the next brother existing at the decease of Shah Aalum. Second, Mirza Ali Kuddar, another son of Jehandar Shah, though not by the same wife. Third, Mirza Jalal-oo-deen. Fourth, Mirza Sulleem-oo-deen. Fifth, Mirza Mahmood Bukht. The three last are sons of the late Mirza Shegoffa Bukht, a son of Jehandar Shah's. All these princes were simply dressed, unassuming in their manner, and of good though plain address. I rose from my seat, met them at the door of the room, embraced them, and handed them to chairs beside me. After a short visit they retired.

August 31st.—I received the visit of Amrut
Rao and his son, Benaick Rao; they came with a
most splendid suwarree of elephants and horses,
till they approached the gate of the paddock in
which Mr. Salmon's house stands; when, in testimony of respect, they got into palankeens, and advanced with only a few attendants. The etiquette
was that I should meet them half-way down the
room, and that (having touched Benaick Rao's
nuzzur) I should embrace them. This being done,
I led them to chairs beside me. They were both
decorated with jewels of extraordinary size and
value. Amrut Rao is brother to the Peishwa, and
was his competitor for the situation. To extin-
guish that claim, and to buy him off from opposition to us, so as to render the termination of the
Mahratta war more easy, Lord Wellesley entered
into engagements with Amrut Rao, that the Company should pay him annually seven lacs of rupees,
until he could be settled in the command of a
territory producing a revenue of that amount; with
a further boon that, till such a territory should be
provided, he should have a camp within the pre-

cincts of which his jurisdiction over his followers should be absolute and unparticipated. This camp has been ever since established in the neighbourhood of Benares. The numbers attached to him have now dwindled to about 5000. Of the tenor of his rule, though he is said to be a good-humoured man, the following instance was mentioned to me. One of his suite, in passing through the bazaar, was attacked by a Brahminy bull; that is to say, by one of those cattle which are dedicated to the gods, and suffered to range at large. The animal struck the man violently in the side, and was preparing to repeat the blow, when the fellow drew his sabre, and gave it a slash across the nose. The circumstance being mentioned to Amrut Rao, he sent for the poor wretch, and had his hand cut off immediately. This is also the ordinary punishment for theft; both hands being in some instances either severed at the wrists, or rendered useless by truncation of the fingers.

I gave to Amrut Rao an English gun of new construction, and to Benaick Rao a recently-invented double-barrelled pistol, with which they

were extraordinarily gratified. In the evening I
felt myself so much recovered, as to be able to take
an airing in the carriage.

September 1st.—I held a durbar, which was
attended by all the principal natives resident at
Benares. First, the Rajah of Benares was introduced anew. As he presented his nuzzur in the
light of a subject of the British Government, I
touched it without rising from my chair; and I
then requested him to accept a khellaut. He was
accompanied by his two brothers. When he
retired to be clothed in the dress, I rose, and went
round the circle. I caused it to be expressed to all
the persons of most weight how sensible I had
been to the polite attention of illuminating the
city for me, desiring that they would communicate
my thanks to their neighbours. Every testimony
of respect is in this country habitually regarded so
much as exacted, and thence requiring no return
of feeling, that this simple acknowledgment on my
part appeared to touch them extremely, and they
showed most lively satisfaction. The Rajah and
Baboo Sheonanain Sing, to whom also I had given
a khellaut, being dressed, were brought forward;

when I put round the neck of each a string of pearls, and delivered to each a scimitar and shield. The presents made by them on this occasion, and which were, as usual, transferred to the collector on the Company's account, were very handsome. I went out again in the carriage this evening. Notwithstanding violent rain, the weather continues uncommonly hot.

September 2nd.—The pundits of the college waited upon me. They showed to me their original Charter from Aurungzebe, and they presented to me a copy (prepared for the purpose) of a most curious historical work preserved among their archives. The writing and the illuminations of this copy were beautiful. I privately directed a present to be given which should overpay its estimated worth. They then produced boys, students in the college, to exhibit their proficiency in the different branches which they were pursuing. Grammar was the first. Two boys sat facing each other on the ground, and in a cadenced tone disputed on the principles of syntax. The dialogue was conducted with an artificial eagerness and quickness that savoured of asperity. Next, a boy

descanted in verse on the basis of medical knowledge. Then, four boys delivered in sing-song
declamation axioms of jurisprudence. Lastly, four
others chanted the fundamental doctrines of religion. As far as powers of memory went, the boys
appeared to be well exercised; but I had learned
that the instruction communicated at this college
was wretchedly superficial in every line. Regretting
that an institution to which there is resort for
education from all parts of India should be so deficient, I have taken those means which the superintendence of Government allows for rendering
this foundation effective for its professed ends;
and I have the satisfaction to believe that the
directions which I have given to a committee for
the purpose cannot fail to put this establishment
on a right footing. The attempt would be hopeless
without the co-operation of some of the principal
natives; but they are so aware of the nullity of
the institution as it now stands, that they wish for
nothing more ardently than to be the active
instruments under the British authority for its
correction and improvement. They are highly
pleased with our advertence to the object. I had

taken a short ride in the morning, and found myself but little fatigued by it.

September 3rd.—I rode again this morning, with sense of benefit. Fearful of not being able to bear the heat of the church, we had divine service performed at Mr. Salmon's. A remarkable proposal was this day made to me. Jyenanain Gocal, a rich native inhabitant of Benares, has begun a considerable building on a lot of ground belonging to him in the suburbs. He desires to make over to trustees, to be appointed by Government, this ground, with the building which he will complete on it, as the establishment of a school for instructing native children in the English language. He proposes to make over at the same time landed property, producing 1,200 rupees annually, and Company's paper yielding interest to the same amount, for the salaries of the English master and his assistants. All that is required by him in return is a pledge, on the part of Government, that the funds shall not be diverted to any other purpose. I have put this into formal train. The disposition to learn English is strong among the natives. Dr. Hare informs me that, before our departure from Calcutta, having found a proper instructor, he had fixed a day school for teaching English to children in the neighbourhood of the Pulta powder-works; and that three young Brahmins had immediately enrolled themselves among the students.

September 4th.—I went to review the troops at the cantonment; two battalions of the 8th, and one of the 12th Native Infantry, with a detachment of the European artillery, the whole under the command of Major-General Wood, of the King's service. Though I was still very weak, I got through it without feeling much fatigued. Prince Mirza Khoorrum was on the field, with four of his sons and two of his brothers. I rode towards him, but there was no making my horse approach the elephants; therefore I was obliged to content myself with sending a compliment to his Royal Highness. When the review was finished, I dismounted in front of the line, and going to the centre of each regiment, caused the native officers to be brought forward and presented to me, as they had not had any other opportunity of being introduced. As soon as this was over, I perceived the prince's elephant at but a little distance, and without remounting, I proceeded towards it. The prince hastened to descend, and came running forward with his children. I embraced him and them, speaking kindly to the latter. The poor man was so intoxicated with this public mark of attention, that I had no sooner quitted him than he entreated Mr. Brooke to give for him to the sepoys one thousand rupees out of his next instalment of stipend. Mr. Brooke very properly apprised me of this, and I put a stop to a liberality so irreconcilable to the narrowness of his Royal Highness's circumstances, making him at the same time comprehend that he had full credit from me for the generosity of the intention. The allowance which he receives from the King of Delhi is very inadequate to his comfortable maintenance. We had scarcely got home before the rain began to fall with prodigious violence. By a whimsical coincidence, the rain, of which the crops had been in serious want, began to fall here on the day of my landing, just as it had done at Monghyr; and nothing would persuade the superstition of the natives that the change of weather was not owing wholly to the fortune of the Governor-General.

September 5th.—Before day-break, we took leave of Mr. and Mrs. Salmon, to whose polished and frank hospitality we felt the truest obligation. We proceeded in our carriages to the city. On our arrrival at the skirts of it, we were forced to get into our palankeens, on account of the narrowness of the streets. The fanaticism of the devotees who resort hither, often subjects Europeans to insult, but we experienced nothing in the crowds but an air of the greatest respect. We first repaired to Prince Mirza Khoorrum's, to visit him and the Sooltana Begum, his mother. The old lady, who is of the best blood of Timoor, is highly respectable. I could see her but indistinctly through the purdah. She put her hand through it, however, soliciting that I would allow her to place that of her son upon mine. Being indulged in this, she said she could now die contented, as she had recommended her son to a protection which she was sure would not prove delusive. I begged the Sooltana to rest satisfied of my dispositions. The prince presented to me a sword of no value, but from its age. It had been Nasr Jung's, and the blade was one of those which ring on being touched by the nail. We thence proceeded to Amrut Rao's. He met us in the midst of his garden, and conducted us to an open hall, admirably calculated for coolness. Fountains which forced the water up in minuter particles than I remember to have seen elsewhere, occupied the front of it. After we had been seated a few minutes and due compliments had passed, Lady Loudoun went to visit the Bhaya, Amrut Rao's wife, while I remained to hear the singing of a couple of nautch girls. Lady Loudoun found the Bhaya and two ladies, who were with her, not at all subjected to the ordinary Hindostanee restraints; for they lifted the purdah and came forward to receive Lady Loudoun, without seeming to mind the gentlemen who accompanied her. On the marches of the Mahrattas the women ride; so that, being at times necessarily exposed to view, they have not that difficulty about showing themselves which is observed by other Hindoo females. While Lady Loudoun was absent, a pretty little girl, his granddaughter, was brought to Amrut Rao, and it was pleasing to see the affection with which he treated her. She was about seven years old, and he told me she had been quite wild with the expectation of seeing the Governor-General. She suffered herself to be embraced with great complacency. On Lady Loudoun's return, magnificent jewels were brought, and earnestly pressed upon us. I referred myself to his knowledge of our customs as my excuse for declining acceptance, but it was with a harder contest that we succeeded in making him comprehend that Lady Loudoun's taking anything valuable would be the same as if I myself received it. He then urged me to accept two elephants and four horses, the latter very fine-looking ones indeed; but he pressed this not in a tone of form, but with a cordial eagerness, which was very well acted if it was not sincere. He implored that I would at least take one horse, which could not be regarded as a valuable article, but as something furnished to me by a Mahratta under obligations to the Company, which might be useful to me in the Company's service. I laughingly said that he should not have to charge me with refusing

everything from him; and I took up a piece of the
stuff which they wind about turbans that happened
to be among the trays of shawls laid before us.
He exclaimed what could I do with it. But he
was perforce satisfied with the answer, that as it
was not for utility, but to keep in remembrance of
him that the article was chosen, it was as sufficient
as any other. During these discussions rose-water
was shot into the air from a syringe with an end
like that of a watering-pot perforated with very
small holes; this, falling like dew, was not unac-
ceptable in a crowded hall. We parted on excellent
terms. Our small boats were waiting for us at a
neighbouring ghaut, to carry us to our vessels,
anchored close to the opposite shore. The city of
Benares, rated as containing about 900,000 fixed
inhabitants, with a fluctuating population of
pilgrims, merchants, &c., estimated at 100,000
more, makes a splendid appearance from the river.
The proportion of houses of good masonry, and of
many stories, is, I believe, greater here than in any
other Indian city. Our vessels were hauled up along
the southern bank of the river till we anchored
close to Ramnaghur, the palace of the Rajah of

Benares, whom we were to visit at night. With round bastions projecting into the water, and various-shaped buildings rising within, this edifice has a picturesque and rather grand appearance. In the evening we went about two miles inland, to see a temple left unfinished by Cheyt Sing. A tank of real magnificence, from size and from the execution of the stone work, stands close to the temple, and is nearly perfect. It is lamentable to see an establishment on which so much money had been lavished abandoned in a state of incompleteness; because it would to future times have been at least a curious monument of the reigning creed of the day. A principle, however, exists among these people never to finish anything begun by a predecessor. They give as a reason for this, that no credit would rest with themselves for the erection, whatsoever might be their amount of expenditure on it; but I rather think there is some unacknowledged fear of ill-luck being entailed by their adoption of an imperfect undertaking. The temple in question is a square building, tall for the extent of its base. It is constructed with the Chunar freestone, which becomes very hard by exposure to the weather. The external sides are divided into compartments containing alto and basso relievos, exhibiting the whole detail of Hindoo mythology. The sculpture is sharp and good; the borders and the friezes, particularly about the doors, display an elegance of pattern which might be well borrowed for our own buildings. This extraordinary assemblage of the symbols of the Hindoo faith bids fair to fall into premature ruin. Much reflection was excited by the contemplation of it. The more I have studied the Hindoo mythology, the more I am convinced of our error in ascribing to it anything of depth or ingenuity. It appears to me a mere tissue of those extravagancies which suggest themselves to all rude and illiterate tribes in their notions of preternatural beings. The phenomena of the climate in which a people exists, viewed as the operation of some superintending spirit, are always likely to determine the features of the prevailing superstition. The marked division of the year in Hindostan into three seasons of equal extent, readily furnished the conception of three tutelary deities, each to preside over his portion of the year. In the four months during which the sun glares through an unclouded atmosphere, the effect of the vivifying ray in calling everything into expansion, activity, and fruitfulness, naturally subministered the idea of a Brahma or creative power as ruler of the teeming season. When this influence of the sun carried to excess had nearly parched everything, the rainy season supervened, refreshed the face of the earth, and restored to the soil the capacity for future exertion, consequences which were easily referred to a Vishnu or preserver. The winter, benumbing, withering, and prostrating the foison of the fields and groves, was aptly delineated as a Siva or destroyer. The interest of the priests, co-operating with this tendency of the mind, substantiated the floating fiction; and thence were instituted rites to those deities, the result of which was to be augmented authority and profit to the Brahminical order. That the worship of this triad should continue unadulterated under the separation of communities was impossible. Each horde that had established itself in a remote or secluded situation gave way to local impressions, to superstitions arising from accidental circumstances, or to flighty imaginations; and so a special god was devised for

the petty district. Then, there was no having a
deity without framing a life and history for him.
Now, people following the same course of habits
were, without any concert, almost sure to fabricate
similar occupations, conduct, and adventures for
their respective gods. In process of time the
augmented population of the country brought the
tribes into contact with each other, and formed a
chain of communication which imposed on the
Brahmins the necessity of adverting to these
various aberrations from the fundamental creed.
The most obvious mode of remedying the mischief,
when the putting any of the tribes under the ban
of heresy might have occasioned their revolt, was
to found on the correspondence of adventures an
assertion that these apparently different divinities
were only Brahma, Vishnu, or Siva, described in
the exertion of some one particular quality out of
the many which they possessed : assuming that, in
consequence, the local name only designated the
peculiar attribute under which the individual of
the triad was worshipped at that place. The in-
consistencies thus induced, such as the identifying
the subordinate gods Crishna and Surga, with the

personages of the triad, while they were kept distinct by the occurrences of their histories, were of small account in the calculation of the Brahmins, who had to deal with a gross and submissive flock. Intercourse, however, with the Chaldeans, probably, subjected the Brahmins to a greater dilemma. The unity of the Supreme Being was a doctrine so sublime, and so congenial to the innate convictions of the heart, that the Brahmins could not directly withhold a recognition of it; yet they would not relax the hold they had obtained over the multitude by their own settled mythology. They therefore endeavoured to reconcile the systems, by declaring that the members of their triad only typified the sole Almighty in the application of one or other of his principal powers. This basis being laid, it was natural, indeed unavoidable, to construe as emblematical the numerous strange portraitures of spiritual beings which irregular or barbarous fancy had generated. We Europeans, setting out with a false notion of the venerable origin of these ancient creeds, have gone beyond the Brahmins in the attempt to give allegorical meanings to that which was but simple absurdity.

We endeavour to form intelligible connexions, and to advance rational solutions for the incoherent extravagancies either in sculpture or story which the antiquities of this country present : forgetting it to be so much the propensity of unenlightened man to run into those distortions, when he wants to describe a being superior to himself, as to make it certain that the North American tribes, or any other race of savages, would with similar advantages of climate, similar facilities for concert in labour, and similar leisure, display an exactly correspondent representation of godheads.   In illustration of this I will specify the explanation which we give of the figure of Vishnu recumbent on the serpent Ananta Naga, or cobra capella, with seven heads.   We translate this representation into a type of the preserving power reposing on eternity. That meaning appears to me wholly gratuitous. Our knowledge that among the Egyptians a serpent with its tail in its mouth (an emblem possibly borrowed from Hindostan) was a hieroglyphic for eternity, has induced us to affix the same sense to the serpent here.   But it was the bending of the serpent into a circle, a form without an end, and not simply its supposed annual renovation of youth by casting its slough, in which the allusion of the Egyptian symbol consisted; and there is not in the Hindoo representation now under discussion any attempt to throw the reptile into that shape, neither can I learn that there exists in this country any supposition of a renewed principle of life attached to a serpent's change of skin. I see nothing in the Hindoo figure but the clumsy conception that, because a cobra capella, with one head, is a formidable animal, a serpent of that kind swelled to gigantic size, and with seven heads, must be proportionally more terrible; so that obviously it must be a divinity alone who could reduce it to subjection to his purposes. In like manner, the serpents twined round the neck and arms of the images of Siva only indicate the celestial properties of the person who could remain unharmed by such noxious ornaments. Since one head furnishes such scope of powers in the human frame, the bestowing four heads on a figure implied a multiplication of faculties, just as the giving four or more arms supposed a commensurate augmentation of strength. These seem to me to be in the lowest class of mental combinations. Sculpture and limning, pursued in a particular mode, may attain a degree of eminence in a country without any concomitant advancement of genius. This has been the case in India. Copies of statues or of pictures were easily made and widely disseminated, so that the rude fantasies received in one quarter were speedily communicated to others; and, as there existed not either taste or science to expose the stupidity of the representations, popular reverence has sanctified them in their original idle forms. Whatsoever the Greeks may have borrowed from this source they at least refined and improved.

As soon as it was dark we proceeded to the Rajah's. According to the arrangement which he had secretly made with Mr. Brooke, we went a considerable circuit in order to approach the palace by the land side. The reason for this was explained when we reached a sort of avenue illuminated on both sides for nearly the length of a mile. The lamps, said to be 70,000 in number, were fixed on frames of bamboo; and, though the plan was simple, the effect was striking. The Rajah received us at a triumphal arch which terminated this approach.   Behind it a large tent was erected under which we were requested to sit and see some fireworks.   When that exhibition was over, we were desired to get into our palankeens, that we might be carried across the two outer courts of the palace.   Those courts were illuminated with blue lights, the vividness of which enabled us to see the oddest mixture of splendour and squalidity around us.   The narrowness of the next door through which we had to pass forbad the entrance of a palankeen, therefore we had to get out and walk. Pieces of flowered silk were spread for us to walk upon; and, as soon as we had passed over them, they were abandoned to be scrambled for by the servants.   This magnificence was singularly contrasted with the narrow passages and stairs through which we now had to pass, where the light of a single small lamp scarcely enabled one to see the way.   When we got to the door of the hall prepared for our reception, pieces of rich brocade spread upon the carpet marked our path to two superb chairs placed on a foot cloth of crimson velvet beautifully embroidered with gold.   These were to be occupied by Lady Loudoun and me.

We could scarcely prevail on the Rajah to sit on a plainer chair beside us. About twenty nautch girls were drawn up in front of us, and sang a congratulatory chorus. After a little while Lady Loudoun went to visit the Rajah's wife in the interior apartment. The nautch girls then sang only two at a time, but without any attempt at a duet after our fashion. It is very remarkable that, when it must be a great object to every one of these girls to show herself off to advantage, female tact has never instructed them to adopt a dress which might display gracefulness of form, or to attempt a dance which might exhibit accuracy of ear and lightness of step. On the contrary, they wear cumbrous trousers which entirely cover the feet; they have a profusion of petticoats with broad fringes, which they seem to be under the continual necessity of hitching up; their only movement is the shuffling forward three or four paces, and then retiring in the same way, sometimes extending a stiff arm with the fingers spread, sometimes bending the arm on the head; and their highest elegance in winning airs appears to be the slipping off and putting up again the part of the mantle or veil which is thrown over the head. There is a perpetual repetition of this last gentility. The natives will sit for hours enjoying this exhibition. To us nothing can be more tiresomely monotonous. On Lady Loudoun's return rich presents of pearls and diamonds were offered, and of course declined. We then took our leave. Both parties were much satisfied; we with the Rajah's efforts to testify respect; he with a visit which gave him distinction in the eyes of his countrymen.

September 6th.—It had been settled that I should shoot this morning at a rumnah or preserve belonging to the Nawab Vizeer. The lagging vessels of the fleet had reached Ramnaghur by the time I got back; when a favourable breeze sprang up and enabled the whole to get across the river. There is no tracking past Ramnaghur; and the current is so strong that any vessel which should have attempted to cross to the opposite bank without a fair and brisk wind would infallibly have been carried far down the stream. We had no sooner got across than the wind failed; heavy rain came on; and at sunset we have tracked no further than to the rumnah, which I had visited in the morning.

September 7th and 8th.—Continuance of violent rain; slow progress and no occurrences.

September 9th.—The rain continued, with excessive heat between the showers. The river ran like a mill-race; so that we did not succeed in getting nearer to Sultanpore than about three miles. Lady Loudoun, going with the children after dark from one pinnace to another, was nearly sunk by a bholiah which had been whirled away by the stream, and had lost all guidance. The cabin of her boat (the *Feel-Cherry*) was beaten in, and her peril was imminent.

September 10th.—Setting off about an hour before daybreak in a very light boat, I reached Sultanpore in time to review the 6th Native Cavalry according to previous appointment. The regiment went through its manœuvres in a way calculated to give me a very favourable impression of the native cavalry. After the review, I breakfasted with Major Houstoun and the officers of the corps. Our vessels having got abreast of the cantonments by the middle of the day, Major-General Wood and a large company dined with us.

September 11th.—Having sent boats forward

during the night for the purpose of crossing the
river to Chunarghur, we set out at four in the
morning, some on horseback and some in palankeens, from Sultanpore.   Embarking soon after
daylight at a ghaut somewhat higher up the river
than the fort which we were to reach, we made our
passage without difficulty, though the stream was
rapid.   As a specimen of an Indian fortress, Chunarghur is interesting, and it is strong.   A hill
within 700 yards of it affords rather too much
facility for raising batteries.   Our chaplain being
on the spot, we had divine service performed, a
circumstance not remembered to have ever occurred
before at the place. We returned readily down the
current to our vessels to breakfast.

September 12th and 13th.—Hot weather, contrary wind, and creeping progress.

September 14th.—Arrived about one o'clock
opposite Mirzapore, the strength of the current
along the steep bank on which the town stands
rendering it undesirable to anchor on that side.
The town, which contains between fourscore and
ninety thousand inhabitants, extends far along the
river, and has a good appearance. At six we went

ashore to dine with Mr. George Ricketts, collector of customs.   Dr. Turnbull, Mr. Sandys, Mr. Patterson, and Mr. Campbell, a merchant, were there introduced to me; as well as a number of military officers.   The town was brilliantly illuminated. After dinner, which had been served in the handsomest style, we returned to our boats.   The rapidity of the stream with which we have had lately to struggle may be best conceived from this fact. It has been ascertained, by the marks of a perpendicular cliff at Mirzapore, that the river fell more than twenty feet in five days.

September 15th.—Sailed from Mirzapore, and anchored at Gungerpoor; not a bad day's work.

September 16th.—Contrary wind and excessive heat.   Reached Coorawan.

September 17th.—Continuation of the same weather.   The Nawab Vizeer has sent to a place in the neighbourhood of Letchiagurry elephants with splendid howdahs, with others for attendants, and richly caparisoned horses, together with tents, palankeens, cooks, and all other accommodations, in case I might wish to go ashore on the left bank of the river.   He has territory there.   We shall probably reach them in the course of to-morrow. Anchored near Churrah.

September 18th.—Had divine service aboard. The heat was oppressive, the thermometer being at 95°, so that we did not make as much progress in tracking as we expected. Anchored about five miles short of Letchiagurry.

September 19th.—Passed Letchiagurry, receiving a salute from two field-pieces attached to a company of the Nawab Vizeer's troops stationed there.

September 20th.—An easterly wind carried us forward briskly, and somewhat cooled the air. We anchored at night about eight miles short of Allahabad.

September 21st.—We anchored close to the fort about mid-day. At five o'clock we landed, and I walked round the works. The fort stands between the Ganges and the Jumna, on a tongue of land which widens speedily from its point; the latter being the position of the fortress. The old rampart to the land side has been taken down, and that face has been regularly fortified on the European system. The works have been made too high, so that the fire from them is plunging overmuch. This is not the most material defect. From an unreflecting adherence to the general principles of fortification, such a portion of the polygon as would extend from river to river was taken for the purpose. Now, in all sieges the ground of calculation on which the certainty of ultimately (unless impeded by interruption or accident) reducing the place rests, is this computation. That as the parallels of the besieger are segments of a larger circle drawn from the same centre than the portion of the fortress to which they are opposed, a greater quantity of artillery can be placed on those parallels to bear on the defences than can be mounted on the latter to annoy the assailant. Thence the probability is, that the fire of the besieger will, from its superiority, dismount the guns of the fort and dismantle the parapet, thereby securing from serious obstruction the formation of the breaching batteries and the subsequent operations from the counterscarp. It follows that on a neck of land suddenly widening from the point on which a fortress is to be placed, such a plan should be adopted for the works as should diminish the advantage an enemy would have in embracing them with his parallel.

After having inspected the fort and complimented the commandant, Colonel Haldane, on the good order in which I found it, we went to take up our residence at the house of Mr. Fortescue, the magistrate, about a mile from the fortress.

September 22nd.—Our boats, which, according to usual process, anchored in the mouth of the Jumna, had been ordered to get round the fort into the Ganges. In the trial three of them perished. The danger of the spot is strongly marked by this incident, because the current was by no means in so formidable a state as is often the case. At daybreak I went to review on the glacis the two companies of artillery stationed here. They satisfied me highly. At twelve o'clock I had a levee for the European officers and civilians. Colonel Frith, with several officers, had travelled all night from Pertaubghur, to pay their attentions. At five in the afternoon I received Prince Jehangeer, who had earnestly solicited to be allowed to see me. He is third son to the King of Delhi, who wished to declare him heir-apparent, but was resisted in that plan by our Government. The young man, naturally of violent temper, was indignant at this opposition, and indulged himself in absurd attempts to raise a party with the view of carrying the matter by force. He was further so insolent to the Resident, and expressed himself in terms which gave so much to be feared for the lives of his brothers, that Government was obliged to interfere, and insist on his being removed from Court. He was accordingly sent hither in a state of honourable exile ; but he behaved so ill, from excessive intemperance in drinking, that it was necessary to threaten him with closer restrictions. When my intention of visiting the Upper Provinces was proclaimed, Prince Jehangeer sent to the magistrate a request for an interview. On Mr. Fortescue's waiting on him, his Royal Highness promised that, if Mr. Fortescue would try to get him received by me, he would behave with the greatest regularity, and would confine himself to one bottle of port wine daily for his own drinking. The magistrate was glad to make the engagement. As the prince had from the date of that agreement conducted himself quietly, I made no hesitation about admitting his visit. When he arrived I rose, and advancing to the door of the room, embraced him, leading him afterwards to a chair beside me. He was in a Tartar dress; the robe crimson satin, the vest blue, both lined with fur, though the weather was overpoweringly hot. On his head he wore a high conical cap ornamented with fur and jewels. His hair was long, and frizzed at the sides just enough to prevent its hanging too lankly on his shoulders. I spoke to him kindly and cheerfully; but he was too agitated and frightened to recover any possession of himself. After a short interval I reconducted him to the door, and he departed with a salute of artillery from field-pieces which I had ordered from the fort. At eight o'clock we partook of a grand dinner, to which Mr. Fortescue had invited all the European officers and civilians, with such of their families as were in the neighbourhood.

September 23rd.—I went early in the morning to return the visit of Prince Jehangeer. Our route lay through the city of Allahabad. It is one long street of mud houses, with every appearance of poverty. About a score of brick houses of two stories, standing here and there, retired some little distance from the street, do not suffice to correct the air of meanness. The prince's residence is within what is here called a garden, that is, a considerable space fenced round, with a few straggling trees in it, but without the slightest attempt at polish. It reminded me of the playground of some of our great schools. The prince occupies a tolerable house in it; and at some little distance there is another for his women. He was a little more composed than he appeared yesterday, but still timid and embarrassed. From his countenance, one might well judge his character. Frowardness and impatience are strongly marked on it, but nothing that indicates real energy. The conversation I addressed to him was calculated to set him at ease; but I suspect that he always thought some austere lecture was coming out. After I got home, I directed that Ahmud Begh should be brought to me from the fort, and he came accordingly under a guard. This was one of the Bundelcund chiefs. He had resisted strenuously our occupation of the province, and had been made prisoner. On giving his parole that he would not attempt anything hostile to the British interest, he had been liberated. Shortly after he collected a body of troops, raised the standard against us, and endeavoured to excite the province to revolt. Being taken a second time, he was sent hither, and had remained as a state prisoner for nine years within the walls of the fort. The perfect order in which Bundelcund now is, renders it quite unnecessary to retain this wretched man in durance any longer from consideration of security, and in point of punishment he had undergone an ample portion. I therefore sent for him to give him his liberty. I announced this to him, apprizing him at the same time that I had ordered five hundred rupees to be paid to him to defray the expense of his journey to his relations. Though, from my sending for him, he had probably anticipated his freedom, the poor creature was so overcome, that he scarcely attempted an expression of thanks. His agitation was such that the perspiration trickled down his face, and his muslin robe was wet through with it in an instant. It was not till he had quitted my room that he recovered himself, shedding tears plentifully, and using the most extravagant expressions of gratitude. In the

middle of the day I held a durbar, at which I conferred a khelaut on Meer Gholam Ali, the vakeel
sent by the Vizeer in charge of the elephants, &c.
In the afternoon I went to look at a battalion of
the 14th Native Infantry, which is in excellent
state. We then proceeded to examine the powder
works. They were little worth inspection; but
some adansonias close to them are curious. As
these trees are not natives of India, they have
probably been brought by pilgrims, who came to
visit Allahabad, replete with objects of veneration,
and who planted them in honour of some one of
the divinities worshipped here. The largest of
these trees is thirty-five feet round. They have
no beauty, the branches being scanty and diminu-
tive in proportion to the trunk. It is only the
bulk of the latter that can attract attention. The
wood is quite spongy. We embarked, after dark,
in our vessels at Pepamow on the Ganges.

September 24th.—So many of the vessels had
got aground in their passage round from the
Jumna, that, had the fleet sailed this morning, we
must have left behind, in irremediable distress,
several of our party. Nothing but the great

quantity of men which could be applied from the fleet to the stranded boats, offered a chance for their relief. Every attention, therefore, was directed to this object. The river, by the official report made to me, has now fallen thirty-nine feet from the highest line which it had attained this year. I went at dawn to the northern bank, to see Meer Gholam Ali's encampment. Everything is in the most magnificent style. The elephants and horses are of the first quality. All the appointments rich and beautiful. This sumptuous establishment includes even beds, which appear no less luxurious than splendid; so that everything was provided in case of my thinking fit to travel by land. In short, the whole thing is done in a manner becoming a great prince, who wishes to mark a peculiar attention. Gholam Ali appears active and intelligent. I understand he was wonderfully flattered by his khelaut, the conferring of which was no less a compliment to the Vizeer than to Gholam Ali. The crews of our boats make a whimsical appearance. I directed that they should all be indulged, in successive parties, with permission to go and bathe at the junction of the

Jumna and Ganges; an observance held of singular efficacy for the purification of a sinner. The bathing, however, is not the whole of the operation. Every person who takes the dip gets his head, whiskers, and eyebrows completely shaven. This business is in the hands of the Brahmins, who make the poor people pay heavily for this smoothing of their persons. Two hundred and fifty thousand pilgrims have been known to come to Allahabad in one year, to go through this ceremony; therefore, it may be calculated that these holy barbers have no bad trade of it. The repairing thus to distant places of worship is strongly inculcated by the Brahmins, who thereby play into each other's hands for reciprocal profit. It should have been mentioned that the report of the number of feet which the river has fallen is not made on loose estimate. The bastion of the fortress, which projects into the water, is graduated for the purpose of showing the exact height of the river. Ahmud Begh came down to the landing-place, dressed as became his former rank, to solicit that he might be allowed to follow me whithersoever I went, desiring to make oath of fidelity on the Koran. I entreated him to hasten to his own connections, and to lose in their society the memory of his sufferings.

September 25th.—We sailed with a strong breeze from the eastward, and ran for about fourteen miles very pleasantly. We then got into a part of the river so full of small banks and shoals, that we could not profit longer by the favourable wind. Six or seven boats were seen stranded at a time, and when one was got off another appeared in the same distress. We were thence obliged to bring-to very early, off a small village called Futtehpore. It stands on a sort of little promontory, which is not high, but resembles a number of hillocks tumbled together. The resistance of this mound to the river is said to arise from the quantity of conca mixed with the earth, which is thereby rendered firmer. The conca is the species of limestone known between this and Calcutta. It never forms a stratum, but is found in detached nodules of rugged appearance, from the size of a pea to that of a lump weighing two or three pounds. Divine service was performed in the *Sonamukhee*.

September 26th.—The shoals made our progress very slow. Boats were getting aground continually.

Mr. Ricketts' pinnace struck upon a shoal, and received such damage that he and his family were forced to quit her. Had she floated off into deep water, she would have gone down. Another vessel bilged in straining against the current, and two of her crew were lost. We anchored between Singhoor and Juklanabad.

September 27th.—The breeze was fair; but a collection of thick clouds in the horizon made us anticipate the equinoctial gale. It came on about noon, and blew heavily, with much rain. Luckily, the wind continued in the right quarter. Some damage was done to sails and masts. We stopped early in the evening, about two miles short of Churrah, in order to let the scattered vessels rejoin us. In the course of the day I received a petition from the Mahomedans of Allahabad, for an object to which they had not adverted when I was on the spot. A mosque of rather elegant structure stands on the esplanade beyond the glacis. When we obtained possession of Allahabad, the proprietary right in the mosque was considered as transferred by the former government to ours; and, from some temporary exigency, the building was filled with stores. These being subsequently removed, much injury, through wantonness or neglect, was suffered by the edifice; and, upon some crude suggestion, our Government had directed it to be pulled down. Fortunately, the intervention of other business had caused the completion of this order to be deferred till next month. The Moslems now implored that the building might be regarded as a monument of piety, and be spared. I have ordered that it shall be cleansed and repaired, and then be delivered over to the petitioners.

September 28th.—We pursued our voyage as soon as it was light; but a turn in the river gave us a direction which rendered the wind foul. It was blowing fresh, and the water was rough, so that we found great difficulty in tracking. The wind soon increased to so hard a gale that the endeavouring to proceed was out of the question; so we anchored off Churrah. Before we brought-to, a small vessel, incapable of bearing the strain of being dragged against wind and stream, bilged close to our pinnace and went to pieces instantly. Three of her crew were in extreme danger from being drawn into the sort of whirlpools formed by the current. Two of them would infallibly have been drowned had it not been for the activity of one of our European servants (Mitchell), who happened to be in a row-boat, and hurried to their assistance. The apathy of several of the natives, who were in row-boats much nearer than Mitchell's, was striking, and very painful to one's feelings.

September 29th.—The storm had continued during the best part of the night; but it lulled in the morning. We got up our anchors, tracking slowly. Passing Marrickpore, where there are some picturesque ruins, we took up our station for the night off Nabobgunge.

September 30th.—The Nawab Vizeer's elephants being close to us, I went ashore at daybreak to beat a jungle which was represented as likely to contain a great quantity of game. We went four miles; but on arriving at the place, we found it so destitute of any cover that there was not a chance of finding anything there. The people are strongly deficient in conception of what is requisite towards sporting, though they are often employed in it. We returned to our boats, and made a tolerable day's progress, considering the wind was unfavourable, and we anchored off Nobuster ghaut.

October 1st.—We advanced slowly. I observed on the shore a man who had been brought down to die by the river-side, and who was apparently dead when we passed. The bed-frame on which he had been carried was close to him. He lay under a coarse cloth, with his head downward, and close to the water, on so steep a slope as that the posture must soon have put an end to his life. Remarking the circumstance to a gentleman of my suite who had resided long in the country, he told me that he had once witnessed with horror the struggles of a wretched old man, probably in a state of hopeless disease, whose pious relatives were endeavouring to smother him by filling his mouth and nose with the holy mud. A short distance in advance, our attention was attracted by a great number of earthen pots heaped on a kind of altar. On inquiry, we found that they had contained ghee, rice, &c., brought as offerings at the self-immolation of a widow who burned herself with the body of her husband. She was a girl of ten years of age. Her husband was but thirteen when he died. By the

Hindoo customs, the girl could not have married again. She would thence have been a burthen to her family, to avoid which they had probably persuaded her to say she would burn herself; and, the profession once made, there is no receding. This miserable child, whose extreme youth could allow her no impulse of real sentiment, was thus subjected to a cruel death from motives of mere convenience. Such are the dreadful consequences which flow from the want of instruction in moral principle among a people peculiarly mild in natural temper! We anchored off Coota.

October 2nd.—Divine service was performed very early on board the *Sonamukhee*. Afterwards we proceeded on our voyage. But we were obliged to anchor off Dalmow, about two in the afternoon, by the coming on of heavy squalls with violent rain.

October 3rd.—No occurrence. Made a moderate advance.

October 4th.—Nothing particular. Gained about eleven miles. At night we reckoned ourselves, by the river, thirty-two miles from Cawnpore.

October 5th.—We attempted to advance by a

nullah which has within these few years been made by the floods through the middle of what Reynell lays down as an island of great extent. We proceeded a considerable way, when we found the channel quite blocked up by shoals, probably formed during the late equinoctial gale. Our pilots having passed the strait but a little while before, we were obliged to return, losing, in fact, our whole day's labour. We anchored off Sirajepore, where the ruinous state of several mosques, ghauts, and other public buildings (some of which had been elegant) excited a painful sensation.

October 6th.—We made a moderate day's work, and anchored close to Nudjeefghur. When I visited Chunarghur, I remarked in the report made to me the name of a person who had been imprisoned there about twenty-two years, in solitary confinement, except for that hour in the day during which he was allowed to walk about under charge of a sentry. All that could be told me was that he had been condemned to death for murder by a court-martial, and that Lord Cornwallis (during his first government) had commuted the punishment into confinement for life. I ordered the proceedings of the court-martial to be sought. It has been found impossible to recover them. And the only record is in the orderly-book at the time, by which the sentence is approved, and so far remitted as that the prisoner, then only fourteen years of age, should be imprisoned for life. It is evident that there could not be the atrocity of deliberate murder in the case, or Lord Cornwallis would never have dispensed with the capital punishment. So that it is to be inferred the homicide was one of those which, though they came under the construction of murder in law, did not so justly stand within the description as to amount to real crime.

Now, for anything short of premeditated murder, twenty-two years of solitary imprisonment must be regarded as an infliction that ought to be considered as having amply chastened the offence. By being a military prisoner, and thence not brought under the eye of the magistrate, the poor wretch has no doubt been overlooked. I have pardoned him on the ground that his crime must be sufficiently expiated by such a length of suffering.

October 7th.—Got forward well, and anchored

at night a little above the ghaut of Janje-
mow.

October 8th.—Landed, and proceeded on horseback, chiefly over a dusty, arid plain, to Cawnpore.
The troops of the cantonment were drawn up
on the race-course, their usual exercising ground.
They consisted of the 24th Light Dragoons, the 5th
Native Cavalry, the 67th regiment, two battalions
of native infantry, and a considerable strength of
Golandauzes, or native artillerymen. I took up
my residence at the house of Mr. Grant, the collector. It is an elegant bungalow, and the grounds
around it are laid out with a degree of taste not
common in India, where individuals always looking
forward to translation to a better post cannot be
expected to lay out money on beautifying a precarious possession.

October 9th.—Sunday.—Went to the church of
the cantonment. It is a simple bungalow of one
room, utterly inadequate to the accommodation of
the troops, or even that of the officers alone.

October 10th.—A review of two brigades of
six-pounders (six guns in each), that I might see
how the oxen worked. The animals exhibited not

only great docility and steadiness, but an activity far beyond what I could have expected. The native officers and men conducted their guns with great precision. The Nawab Vizeer arrived this morning in his camp about a mile on the other side of the bridge of boats, which had been thrown over the Ganges to facilitate our communications.

In the afternoon his Excellency sent his son Nusser-oo-Deen to compliment me, and to propose the Nawab Vizeer's waiting upon me the next morning. I prevailed on Nusser-oo-Deen to stay and dine with me. He is a very unaffected, interesting boy, about thirteen years of age. Our frank kindness to him appeared to make a strong impression. The Resident, Major Baillie, accompanied him to his father's camp after dinner.

October 11th.—The Nawab Vizeer came to breakfast. I received him with all possible cordiality. His countenance is mild and good, though not betokening energy. The fashion in which he wears his beard, very grey, though he is scarcely more than forty, is singular. It is just in the state that the beard of one of us, in the habit of shaving, would exhibit if left untouched for a week. And this is the case with his upper lip, as well as with the rest. He ate of everything that was offered to him. A number of his brothers attended him, as did also Nusser-oo-Deen, who is his only son. The latter assumed all the freedom of former acquaintance, but with perfect respect and good breeding. I gave to him a beautiful wrought Highland dirk, a present with which he seemed much delighted. The Nawab Vizeer took his leave, and departed amid the salute from field-pieces which I had caused to be brought into Mr. Grant's paddock for the purpose. Another brigade of our guns saluted him on his elephant's entering on the bridge. In the afternoon I went to examine the ordnance-yard. I found it in a state which did the highest credit to Colonel Grace, who superintends the field depôt. I had some time ago written to have some howitzers mounted in a particular manner for service in the Nepaul Hills. It is difficult to convey one's notions accurately in writing, where one has to describe a thing of which no pattern has previously existed. Colonel Grace had caught my conception so exactly as that I found the carriages of the howitzers precisely what I wished.

The gun wheels can be taken from the body of the carriage within one minute, so as that the pieces are severally portable (slung on bamboos) by ordinary porters; the howitzer can be remounted with equal dispatch. These pieces of ordnance must therefore be extraordinarily useful for service in a mountainous country. Its principal advantage is, that it throws the shrapnel-shell of a 12-pounder.

October 12th.—The oracles of established etiquette represented, that were I to return the visit of the Nawab Vizeer the very day after that on which he had come to me, it would be a distinction beyond his relative rank. I was, therefore, obliged to let this day intervene. I employed it in reviewing the 24th Light Dragoons, commanded by Colonel Need. They are 800 strong; and I have had the satisfaction of finding them in the highest state of discipline. Major Baillie informed me that the Nawab Vizeer had taken to himself the dirk which I had given to his son, saying it was too handsome for a boy to wear.

His Excellency had been highly gratified with the manner in which he was received by me.

October 13th.—I set out early to return the visit of the Nawab Vizeer. On crossing the bridge of boats and setting foot on his territory, I was saluted by cannon advanced from his camp for the purpose; and a party of his bodyguard, as well as some shutar sowars (camel-troopers) joined themselves to my escort.

Among the camels were some which carried a swivel gun pointed backwards, so that, in covering a retreat, it is fired without interruption to the progress of the camel. The effect must be very uncertain. The camp was straggling and irregular; and no attention appeared to have been paid to order further than the reserving a clear road to the Nawab's tents. His Excellency, encompassed by a prodigious and confused swarm of attendants, met me at some distance from them. We managed, after the formal salaams, to shake hands off our respective elephants, and then proceeded side by side. A sort of squealing instrument, which sounds very like the twopenny trumpets of children in England, announced the elevated characters which it preceded. Alighting within the court of the tents—a large space encircled by a canvas wall of ten feet in height,—we entered the durbar tent.

There were two rich chairs placed at the end of the room, on a carpet of crimson velvet, finely embroidered. One of the chairs had been purposely made more splendid than the other, and his Excellency obliged me to seat myself in it. All the members of his family were then brought up, as well as the other principal persons of his court, to be presented. I had duly received my lesson as to this ceremonial, in which a most pointed difference is made, according to the rank of the individual —some being met by rising and embracing them; others being suffered to put their foreheads to your knee as you continue sitting, and to be only marked by putting the hand on their shoulder as a kind of inferior embrace; while another class are only to make their obeisance at a distance. Nautch girls were then summoned, who sang for a short time in their usual uninteresting manner. Breakfast was then announced. It was served in a vast tent, and very commodiously disposed. A happy mixture of the English and the Hindostanee taste made the breakfast excellent.

When the Nawab Vizeer breakfasted with me he said he looked up to me as a father. I said laughingly, in return, "Then I am to consider this young man (his son) as my grandson, and, of course, to feel pledged to his support."

Adverting to that speech, Nusser-oo-Deen on the present occasion asked after the health of his grandmother, meaning Lady Loudoun. I answered that he did right in using the expression, for if he had confidence enough in us to claim parental care, he should not be disappointed. This declaration appeared to make a strong impression on those present. After breakfast I desired to speak to the Nawab Vizeer apart. He took me to a retired tent, accompanied by Mr. Ricketts and Mr. Swinton, whom I had desired to be present, as well as Major Baillie. When we were seated I addressed the Nawab Vizeer at some length on my view of the character which the relation of the two states ought to bear; I explained that the leaving of him perfect freedom of action in his internal administration of his dominions was the principle on which I meant to proceed; I assured him that there was not, on the part of the

British Government, the remotest notion of further circumscribing his territories; I professed it to be my wish to attach to his station all the dignity and the authority requisite to give it lustre and influence in the eyes of his family and subjects; and I closed by entreating him to place unbounded reliance in the Resident, Major Baillie, as that gentleman possessed my entire confidence. There were points in this address to which the Nawab Vizeer appeared very sensible. But at the termination there was such a deficiency of any show of gratification that I was much struck with his manner. I ascribed it, however, to Asiatic reserve. His Excellency thanked me politely for my dispositions; expressed his knowledge that the musnud of Oude must rest wholly on the protection and justice of the British Government; affirmed that he could never have the notion of a discrimination of interests; and said he had looked forward with eager solicitude to this day as the period which would put an end to all the misunderstandings whence the last years of his father had been made unhappy. He added that he had put into writing some points for my consideration, and entreated that I would weigh them favourably. He then put a paper into my hand. As it was in Persian, I delivered it to Mr. Swinton, saying that as soon as a translation should be made, I would peruse it with the most serious attention. Major Baillie could not conceal evident surprise and un-easiness at this occurrence. His bewilderment made him forget himself so far as to take the paper out of Mr. Swinton's hands and to begin to peruse it. I stopped this by observing that it was immaterial to examine the contents of the paper at the moment, as no sudden answer ought to be given on such a subject. Here the conference ended. Returning to the tent, where we had left the company, we found a splendid present of trays of jewels and shawls laid out. I declined them. But I accepted a sword, richly set with diamonds, which had been made on purpose for me. The expediency of giving the Nawab Vizeer entire con-fidence in me made it requisite that I should induce him to believe I had taken this gift; though I subsequently in secret lodged with the public secretaries an acknowledgment of its being the sole property of the Honourable Company, and to be delivered to them after I should have gone through the expected ceremony of wearing it at Lucknow. Swords enamelled after the Lucknow fashion were presented to the secretaries and to my aides-de-camp, which I allowed them to take, as it was understood to be a compliment offered by the Nawab Vizeer on his accession to the musnud. We then repaired to the tent in which we had been seated before breakfast. Two fine horses and the noblest elephant I had ever seen were brought to the door for my acceptance. The elephant was of a prodigious size and excellent shape. It carried an ombara (a howdah, covered with an elevated dome, and only used by sovereigns) of extraordinary magnificence. These articles were pressed upon me by the Nawab Vizeer with the keenness of urgency, in which his brothers and sirdars earnestly joined. At length, by way of enforcing his request, he said one of the horses was the favourite of his father, who had destined it for me. Glad to compound the matter, I said so flattering an attention of the deceased Nawab should not fall to the ground; and that I would take that horse in the hope that the Nawab Vizeer would accept

from me as a curiosity a machine for making ice,
which I had brought from England. The Nawab
Vizeer continued to urge my acceptance of the
elephant on account of its extraordinary bulk
and its tried steadiness in tiger-hunting; but
on that point I remained inflexible. We then
separated. A Mr. Clarke, in the service of
the Nawab Vizeer by licence from government,
had been recommended to my secretary, Mr.
Thomson, as a person whose local knowledge as
well as established integrity might render him
useful to Mr. Thomson in any of his arrangements
for the household while we should be at Lucknow.
This gentleman was invited to dine with me to-day,
as was also Captain M'Leod, of the Company's
Engineers, who had been lent to Saadut Ali to
superintend the construction of some buildings,
and had been retained in that employment by the
present Nawab. When they arrived at Mr. Thomson's tent before the hour of dinner, by way of
something to say, he expressed his satisfaction at
thinking that what I had explained to the Nawab
Vizeer must have made his Excellency quite happy.
To his astonishment, they answered that so far

from his being happy, they had left the Nawab in a state of absolute despair.   On his asking with much surprise the cause, they told him that the Nawab Vizeer had reckoned on being emancipated from the imperious domination of Major Baillie, under which his Excellency groaned every hour, but that I had professed my confidence in Major Baillie, and had riveted him in his position.   Mr. Thomson lost no time in apprizing me of this extraordinary communication, which he justly thought ought not to be withheld from my knowledge.   I sent for the two gentlemen separately, and questioned them on the point.   It was clear that the Nawab had imparted to them all I had said, for my very expressions were repeated by them, and no attendant of the Nawab's had been present at the conference, so they must have had the information from himself.   They concurred exactly in what they stated as his observations on my language.   On my declaring that the confidence in Major Baillie, professed by me, was a compliment paid to the Nawab, whom I imagined entertained a peculiar predilection for the Resident, they severally exposed the reasons of the Nawab's disgust.

They stated that his Excellency considered the assistance afforded to his tranquil possession of the musnud to have been rendered by the Resident in his official capacity on the part of the British Government; and though his Excellency felt obligation to the instrument, still it was not of an amount to counterbalance the grievous dissatisfactions which he daily experienced. He complained that Major Baillie dictated to him in the merest trifles, broke in upon him at his palace without notice, whensoever he (the Resident) had anything to prescribe, fixed his (Major Baillie's) creatures upon his Excellency with large salaries, to be spies upon all his actions; and above all, lowered his Excellency in the eyes of his family and his subjects by the magisterial tone which he constantly assumed. I asked why the Nawab Vizeer had not unfolded this to me when I pressed him so distinctly to mention what would contribute to his comfort. The reply of each of them was that the Nawab's mind was in a state of such subjugation to Major Baillie that his Excellency did not dare to hint at a dissatisfaction before him. To both I testified my disappointment at finding I had failed in my earnest wish of making the Nawab's situation essentially agreeable as well as ostensibly dignified; but I did not hint at anything I had in contemplation.   Here the conversation ended.

October 14th.—Reviewed his Majesty's 67th Regiment, commanded by Lieutenant-Colonel Huskisson. It was in excellent order. Received a letter from Mr. Clarke, in which he states his having related to the Nawab Vizeer my expressions of surprise at the Nawab's want of frankness towards me, and communicates his Excellency's solicitation that I would indulge him with a private interview when he came to dinner with me next day. Mr. Ricketts was requested to answer this letter; to say that the Nawab should have a conference without Major Baillie's being present; but to desire Mr. Clarke to address any future communications through the regular channel of the public secretaries. In the evening, I visited the school of the 67th Regiment. It was perfectly well-conducted; and I learned with great pleasure that several natives were anxious to send their children thither for instruction.

October 15th.—The Nawab Vizeer met me on

the review ground soon after it was light. He approached with a prodigious crowd of attendants. A loose mob of spearmen and torch-bearers ran before his elephant; so far from aiming at any regularity, they obviously studied the contrary by frequently running across each other. The appearance of bustle is thereby increased, and this is according to their notions a fit appendage to dignity, nor is that conception quite erroneous, for the confusion seems to multiply the swarm and gives an air of excessive interest in what they are about. Their clamour was as vehement and as unceasing as their motions. After the interchange of compliments, I stationed the Nawab where he might best see the manœuvres to be executed. The troops were the King's 24th Light Dragoons, the 3rd Native Cavalry, a troop of Horse Artillery, two strong brigades of Foot Artillery, the King's 67th Regiment, two battalions of Native Infantry, and a small battalion of Golandauzes (native artillerymen) acting in the line with small arms. The troops performed very well. After the review, the Nawab came to breakfast with me, bringing several of his brothers and kinsmen. He expressed surprise and gratification at the exhibition which he had just witnessed. We separated early, as he was to come again at 6 o'clock. Pretty punctually at that hour he arrived, when I immediately said aloud that I wished to have a conference with his Excellency; and I observed to Major Baillie, as if from a sudden thought, that it would be more delicate for him not to be present. I took the Nawab into a private room. I requested Mr. Ricketts, Mr. Adam, and Mr. Swinton to accompany us. I explained that these were principal functionaries of the Government, sworn to secrecy, who would have to settle all the details of whatever might be transacted between the Nawab Vizeer and me, and who might therefore as well hear the business in the first instance; adding that my position made it incumbent on me to lay down the rule of never having an interview with any native prince without the presence of one or other of them.

The Nawab said there could be no objection. I asked if he wished to have any of his own suite present, but he declined it. Before I could open any subject to him, he addressed me, and said that as we were engaged in a war which might embarrass our finances, he begged leave to offer a present of a crore of rupees to the Honourable Company. This was expected by me. I knew that his father had intended to make this offer, in order to mark his gratitude for my having treated him as a gentleman; though I feel that I did nothing more than was demanded by positive justice. The Resident had given me a hint that the present Nawab, aware of his father's intention, had mentioned his purpose of carrying it into effect. I thanked the Nawab cordially for this proof of his attachment to our Government; I said that it was impossible for the Company to accept the sum as a gift, but I professed that I should entertain a very high sense of obligation in receiving it as a subscription to the six per cent. loan now opened by the Council. On that footing the matter was agreed. Nothing could be more opportune, for this command of ready cash emancipated the Government from many urgent financial difficulties. I said to the Nawab that his own consciousness of the way in which I must regard so essential a service, rendered to my administration, ought to make him speak to me with perfect confidence. I assured him that I considered it no less my official duty than it was my personal inclination to make his authority efficient, and his private position satisfactory. I thence entreated that he would explain to me without disguise his wishes. Notwithstanding this encouragement he appeared unaccountably reserved. He said there were facts about which he was solicitous, and that he had put them down upon paper, but he had not brought the paper with him. This singular reserve made me begin to doubt if he had really desired the conference. I therefore asked him if he had authorized Mr. Clarke to request this interview for him, and to make it a condition that Major Baillie should not be present. He answered in the affirmative to both points. I then begged that he would take all the advantage he could wish of the opportunity, and I repeated my assurance that he might rely on my solicitude to gratify him. He said again and again that he had deemed it better to commit his wishes to writing, that he would send the paper on the morrow, that he had the firmest reliance on my kindness, and that he referred me for any explanations to Mehdy Ali Khan. After much time thus vainly spent we went to dinner. At length he departed, expressing his impatience to see me at Lucknow, and taking his leave till that meeting should happen.

October 16th.—Sunday.—We had divine service and communion at the church.

October 17th.—Reviewed the first battalion of the 10th Native Infantry, which is to be my escort on the march. Its steadiness and accuracy did credit to Lieutenant-Colonel Adams, the very respectable officer who commands it.

October 18th.—Examined chevaux de frise and scaling-ladders made by Colonel Grace, according to suggestions which I communicated to him. They were perfectly well executed. I ordered 2000 yards of the chevaux de frise to be prepared. The Nawab Vizeer having insisted that fourteen of his elephants, with howdahs, should attend me to Lucknow, I distributed them accordingly among the gentlemen of the suite.

October 19th.—Reviewed the 5th Native Cavalry, which I found in very good order. I directed that a detachment of it, equal to a troop, should reinforce

my bodyguard for the march along the frontiers.
Lieutenant Ward is to command this party, and
the regiment is to enlist supernumeraries to the
amount of this deduction. In the afternoon I
reviewed Captain Haye's corps of Golandauzes.
They made an excellent show, both with the field-
pieces and small arms.

October 20th.—Our intended march was delayed,
the Nawab Vizeer not having made such progress
in his route as had been expected.

October 21st.—Marched to Ennow, through a
sandy uncultivated tract, for the most of the way.
Distance, eight miles, six furlongs.

October 22nd—Marched to Rhimutgunje; twelve
miles, five furlongs. The country well tilled and
apparently flourishing.

October 23rd.—To Noclgunje, eleven miles,
three furlongs; fine country. Divine service.

October 24th.—To Boodleeka Tuckeen, nine
miles, two furlongs. This position is within five
miles of Lucknow. The whole country, from
Cawnpore hither, is a dead flat; but for the most
part very rich. The Nawab Vizeer sent his son to
meet us on our arrival at our ground, and to stay

with us.   By our having a double set of tents,
one was always sent forward during the night, and
was pitched immediately after daybreak.   We
could therefore offer the young Nawab a comfortable breakfast.   He and his attendants expressed
themselves much surprised at the regular order in
which our camp was laid out, and still more at the
tranquillity which reigned in it.

October 25th.—We moved early towards the
city.   The Nawab Vizeer met me about two miles
from it, and descended from his elephant.   I
quitted mine also; and after embracing him I got
with him upon another elephant equipped with a
magnificent howdah calculated to carry us both.
This was the established etiquette.   In this manner
we proceeded to the city.   The approach to it has
nothing striking.   Within it has a better appearance than any other town I have seen in India.
The wealthier inhabitants were all in their holiday
clothes on the flat tops of their houses.   The
various and lively colours of their shawls had a
pleasing effect.   I had been apprized that on this
public entry I must scatter money to the populace,
as the Nawab Vizeer would do it to those on his

side of the elephant. A bag containing 1000 rupees had been prepared for me accordingly; it may easily be conceived what confusion arose in the narrow crowded streets from the scramble occasioned by this silver shower. An ostentatious liberality of this sort is practised on similar occasions by all the Indian sovereigns. The Nawab Vizeer, to gain popularity on his accession, made it a practice to throw more or less in this manner among the crowd every day he went abroad. He now finds the inconvenience of having introduced the custom, for the people pursue him with clamours if he forbear to make the expected donation. This is not the only mischief of the habit. It tends to brutalize the lower classes in such a degree that I would on no account admit the practice in any of our cities. Several of the gentlemen who were towards the rear of our cavalcade told me that they saw shocking instances of ferocity in the attempts of individuals to wrest rupees from those who had been fortunate enough to catch them. Three or four stout young men were beating a helpless old wretch unmercifully with switches to make him yield his prize. A woman to secure a rupee which she had caught put it into her mouth, and a set of fellows were seen to grasp her throat, and squeeze it till the agonies of strangulation forced her to open her jaws. There was something exceedingly striking in the caution of the elephants not to trample upon the people, who were continually thrown down before them. Where they could not otherwise step clear, they would remove the fallen with their trunks. A horse having taken alarm in the crowd, and becoming riotous, the rider fell off, on which the elephant that carried one of my children and the governess, without any apparent direction from its driver, lifted the man by his arm with his trunk, and raised him till he scrambled into his saddle. It is possible that the elephant might have been previously taught the trick; but its readiness of applying its lesson would even in that case be remarkable. As we proceeded, nautch girls in their gaudiest habiliments sang congratulatory verses from the tops of the houses, with which we were generally on a level. Persons every now and then ran to meet us, throwing up into the air a number of live quails; a pretty compliment, as it was understood to mean a liberation of prisoners on the joyful occasion. We were long in reaching the palace, which is at the further extremity of the town. It does not aim at anything splendid, yet the number of courts through which one passes gives it an air of considerable magnificence. Judgment with regard to display was manifest in the stationary elephants in one court; camels with their riders in another; cavalry in a third; and so on, varying the nature of the guard. At the door of the inner court but one we quitted our elephants, as the passage was too narrow for them.

We proceeded in splendid palankeens to the steps which lead up to the Sovereign's apartments, whither we ascended. They are convenient, neat rooms, in the English style, without attempt at grandeur. In one of them which overlooked the Goomty river, there was a musnud, formed like a long European court, raised on a platform of three steps. Both the musnud and the platform were covered with velvet, and the borders of the former were thickly embroidered with pearls, and with precious stones of a secondary rate. The Nawab Vizeer obliged Lady Loudoun and me to occupy the centre places.   On each side of us sat the two brothers of the King of Delhi, who reside at Lucknow. The Nawab Vizeer himself was at the extremity of the couch.   The brothers of the King of Delhi had come out of the city to meet us, and had accompanied us to the palace, which they never enter as visitors to the Vizeer. Their presence was therefore an attention to the Governor-General. Mirza Sultan Mahommed, a Persian prince of royal lineage, who resides at Lucknow, on a pension from the Company, had similarly come out to meet me, and repaired with us to the palace. He now seated himself on the musnud, at the further extremity from the Nawab Vizeer. The master of the ceremonies exclaimed that it was impossible to allow of his sitting there.   Others of the principal people of the Court went up to him and told him his assuming such a station was wholly inadmissible. The poor man attempted to maintain his ground; but they roundly told him that if he did not descend immediately they would drag him from his seat. He then started forward; desired it should be remembered that he had never once since his being at Lucknow condescended to visit the

Vizeer, and that his being at that moment in his Excellency's palace was only through his duty of attending on me.   He then retired in great indignation.   The Nawab Vizeer, through the whole of this scene, preserved the most immovable steadiness of countenance, as if nothing that passed was either seen or heard by him.   The kinsmen of the Nawab and principal persons of the Court were then brought up to be presented to me and Lady Loudoun.   Breakfast being announced, the Delhi princes took their leave, and the rest of us proceeded under an awning to the banqueting-house. This is a building in the Saracenic taste, light and elegant, without being deficient in richness of ornament, and very commodious.   Tea and coffee, with pillaws, Hindostanee cakes of various kinds, and ices of several sorts, formed an excellent repast. Nautch girls sang during the breakfast.   Some of the voices were deemed of the first rate; but my ear is not fashioned as yet to a falsetto imitating exactly the tone of the instrument which accompanies the singer.   After breakfast, in our way to our palankeens, trays with jewels and fine shawls were laid out and pressed upon our acceptance.   I reminded the Nawab that this ceremony had already been gone through between us, and that we ought now to consider ourselves as too professedly leagued in friendship to give room for this form. On that account, I said with gaiety, I would take his hand instead of his present. This has put a stop to a ceremonial inconvenient to both parties, as etiquette would otherwise have required that on every visit that passed between us the person visited should give the expensive present of thirty-one trays to the other. From the palace we went to the Resident's. The gateway of the latter's compound, as the little paddock surrounding the better style of houses is called in India, is not a bow-shot from that of the palace. With the incongruity which attends everything in this country, the ground between the two (except the beaten road) is all in rough ridges and mounds. I have gone into minute observations, because it is from lesser circumstances that the difference of habits and manners is often best exhibited. At the Resident's I held a levee for the civilians and European officers of the subsidiary force. We dined with Major Baillie. The Nawab Vizeer came to dinner, and seemed unaffectedly to relish being with us. At night we proceeded to Constantia, which is to be our residence. It is three miles from the palace.

October 26th.—I went in the morning as soon as it was light to shoot in the Park of Dilkoosha (soother of the heart), according to a solicitation made to me by the Nawab Vizeer. He pays great attention to anything which he regards as having been the wish of his father. The latter, on its being fixed before his decease that I should inhabit Constantia during my stay in the neighbourhood of Lucknow, had a gate made in the wall of Dil-koosha, opposite to one out of the Park of Constantia, that I might have the convenience of sporting in the former. The parks are divided only by a road. That I might be the more at liberty for my exercise, the Nawab Vizeer would not join the party, but sent his dogs. The amusement was but moderate, as I would not comply with his Excellency's entreaty that I should shoot at the deer and antelopes. We brought home a few partridges and pea-fowl. The park is scarcely more than three miles round. It is thickly wooded, with a quantity of reeds and of a coarse grass which rises to the height of seven or eight feet.

The house, built in the English style, stands upon a gentle elevation with some extent of lawn about it. On returning to Constantia I had the opportunity of considering that mansion. It was erected by General Martyn, a native of Lyons in France, who came to India as a private soldier. Having got into the service of Asoph-oo-Dowlah, he distinguished himself by his talents so as to obtain rapid promotion; but his strict accuracy to punctuality in all pecuniary concerns was more beneficial to him. His character in that respect became so established that all the natives who had amassed money and dreaded the rapacious gripe of the sovereign, entrusted their riches to the care of General Martyn. Such amplitude of funds enabled him to take advantage of many favourable opportunities, and to make many advantageous speculations, so that he gathered extraordinary wealth. He expended some of it in erecting this house on a plan entirely his own. The idea of it was probably taken from those castles of pastry which used to adorn desserts in former days. The mansion consisted of three stories gradually diminishing in the size of the square, so as to leave to the two upper stories a broad space between the apartments and the parapet, which covered the wall of the story below it. This was for the purpose of defence, with a view to which the building was constructed. The doors of the principal floor were plated with iron, and each window was protected by an iron grate. Loopholes from passages above gave the means of firing in perfect security upon any persons who should force their way into these lower apartments. The spiral stone staircases were blocked at intervals with iron doors; in short, the whole was framed for protracted and desperate resistance. The parapets and pinnacles were decorated with a profusion of plaster lions, Grecian gods, and Chinese figures, forming the most whimsical assemblage imaginable. Still, the magnitude of the building, with its cupolas and spires, gave it a certain magnificence. In a vault beneath it is the tomb wherein General Martyn is buried. The figures of four European soldiers resting on their firelocks surround it; and there are lights constantly burning in the room. The general left an estate in trust to defray this expense, and to keep the house in repair for the accommodation of any visitor of rank who might come to Lucknow. There is not much lodging in proportion to the extent of the building, but the state rooms are handsome. The Nawab Vizeer had sent furniture thither from his exuberant magazines, so that we did not find a want of any convenience. The park is only a paddock in which our camp was pitched. The Nawab Vizeer came to breakfast with us, and invited us to dine with him the next day.

October 27th.—The Nawab Vizeer sent two carriages of his own invention, drawn by elephants, to be inspected by us. The notion is dignified. The animals draw the carriages perfectly well. The vehicles are very grand, and would make a fine show in those kind of processions for which they are intended. The Nawab Vizeer has a great mechanical turn. The objection to this invention is, that the carriages could not go through the city of Lucknow, or any other Indian town which I have seen, without tearing down many of the frail mansions which border the narrow streets. In the evening we set out to dine with the Nawab Vizeer.

Illuminations were prepared, and they certainly were beyond anything of the kind I have elsewhere witnessed. With a delicate attention, lamps had been forborne to be placed within the park of Constantia; that being considered as too exclusively ours to be meddled with. But as soon as we got out of its gates we saw the whole road towards the palace bordered with posts, on each of which many lights were fixed. As we approached the palace triumphal arches of lamps, raised on bamboo frames, had an elegant and most brilliant appearance. Proceeding further, we came to a place where, on each side, there were, in transparencies, the representation of a bazaar or market. The costumes of Hindoos and Chinese were strikingly portrayed. Thence we approached a kiosk, or summer-house, decorated with lamps in a manner extraordinarily tasteful. But all this splendour faded in comparison with what opened upon us when we came to a sort of esplanade before the windows of the banqueting-room. It was as large as a middling-sized field in England. The whole of it was laid out to imitate a parterre of flowers. The number of lamps with which the ground was covered for this purpose must have been immense, and the disposition of their various colours, to render the representation accurate, was very happy. We entered the palace at the private apartments, sat on the musnud till dinner was announced, and then repaired to the banqueting-room. The dinner was excellent, but the wine marvellously bad. This might have been expected at the table of a Mussulman host, only it is known that his Excellency had much relish for wine, and used to indulge in it freely, till his father exacted from him an oath to leave off drinking it. One may infer, from the quality of the liquor at present, that the vow is rigidly kept. Nautch girls sang in their usual strain during the dinner. When we rose from table, we went to a large kind of balcony which commanded the illuminated parterre above mentioned. Fireworks were then exhibited in profusion. Few of them were equal to what are seen in Europe. It was late before we got back to Constantia.

October 28th.—We went to Moosa Baugh, a villa of the Nawab Vizeer's about seven miles from Lucknow.

October 29th.—We went soon after it was light

to meet the Nawab Vizeer at Dilkoosha, where
we were to see cheetas run at antelopes.   When
all this was over, we went to examine the interior
of the house.   It was very neatly fitted up in the
European fashion, with English prints in every
room.   The Nawab Vizeer returned with us to
Constantia, and breakfasted there.   Letters from
the Council in Calcutta gave us the intelligence of
the peace in Europe.

October 30th.—We had divine service at Constantia, attended by several of the officers and
ladies of the cantonment.   After prayers, Captain
Gilbert,* Barrack-Master of Cawnpore, desired to see
me.   He had been with us at Dilkoosha the day
before; and I had heard the Nawab Vizeer ask
him to breakfast at the palace this morning.
Captain Gilbert imagined this to be a compliment
on account of his having had much acquaintance
with his Excellency before his accession, and after
we had returned from the park, he asked if I had
any objection to his taking one of my aides-de-
camp (Captain M'Ra) with him.   This I mention
to show how little he could suspect any political

* Afterwards Sir W. R. Gilbert, Bart.

purpose had prompted the Nawab's invitation. It
suddenly struck me to say to him, "As you are
intimate with the Nawab, I wish you would try
to find out, without giving him ground to suspect
the inquiry to come from me, whom it is he wishes
for his physician." I did not explain my motive
to Captain Gilbert. It was this: Mr. Clarke,
among the Nawab's grievances, had stated Major
Baillie's attempt to force upon his Excellency
Major Baillie's own physician (Mr. Wilson), instead
of Mr. Law, who had been physician to his Excellency's father. Major Baillie had, at Moosa Baugh,
told me it was the Nawab's wish to have Mr.
Wilson nominated his physician, and solicited that
I would give my sanction. Doubtful of its being
his Excellency's own desire, I answered that I
would consider of it. And I thence sought the
opportunity of ascertaining the point by means of
Captain Gilbert. The latter now informed me
that after their breakfast the Nawab had requested
to speak to him in a private room. While his
Excellency was looking round that apartment,
apparently to see that all the doors were safe, and
that nobody could overhear, Captain Gilbert, as if

it had been the thought of the moment, asked who was the person whom his Excellency wished to have for his physician.   The Nawab instantly said, " Dr. Law, to be sure !" and he thence began to complain bitterly of the Resident's attempt to force his own protégé on his Excellency.   He proceeded to expatiate with great earnestness on the misbehaviour of Major Baillie towards him, recapitulating precisely the points which had been mentioned by Mr. Clarke.   He said he was in despair at my having said that Major Baillie had my confidence, for that he could never be happy or respectable in the eyes of his subjects while that gentleman should be at Lucknow.   He terminated the conversation by saying that he had been most anxious to unbosom himself on these particulars to Captain Gilbert.   The latter asked why his Excellency did not speak to me frankly on the subject.   His answer was, that he was afraid.   Captain Gilbert has very justly thought it his duty to communicate to me this singular conversation.

October 31st.—This morning I set out to review the two battalions of the Company's infantry at the cantonment about two miles beyond the bridge

over the Goomty. The Nawab Vizeer was to accompany me.   When I arrived at the door of the
palace, which was in my route, I found his Excellency preparing to get into his carriage. As I
was alone in a phaeton, my horses having been sent
forward to the field, I proposed to the Nawab to
accompany me in that carriage, which he accepted.
On the way I said to him that Captain Gilbert
had repeated to me what his Excellency had said of
his wish to have Mr. Law as his physician, adding
that it should be so arranged. He clasped my
hand eagerly, and said that he had no comfort but
in my kindness. The review went off very well.
His Excellency and I returned in the same howdah
to the Residency, where we breakfasted. In the
afternoon I went with Lady Loudoun to see the
Imaum Bareh. It is a truly magnificent and
elegant building, consisting of two quadrangles, on
one side of the interior of which stands a mosque,
a really noble fabric. The principal hall of the
building contains the tomb of Asoph-Oo-Dowlah.
It is a grave of earth sodded, the pavement being
in that part interrupted for the purpose. A canopy
of cloth of gold, embroidered with verses of the

Koran, in black silk, covers it.   This canopy is
supported by elevated gilt pillars.   Festoons of
fragrant flowers are suspended from it, and little pots
of incense are burning around.   Bands of priests,
which relieve each other at stated periods, chant
day and night passages of the Koran at the head
of the grave.   Everything is in the highest order,
though it must be difficult to keep the place clean,
from the multitude of pigeons which haunt it, and
which I understand are to be on no account dis-
turbed.   Both Mussulmans and Hindoos attach a
character of sanctity to any animals which take up
their abode near places deemed sacred.   The Nawab
Vizeer came to dinner with us at the Residency,
and appeared much gratified by our having been
to visit the Imaum Bareh.   In consequence of what
Captain Gilbert had told me, I had sent Mr.
Ricketts to the Nawab this morning to entreat
that his Excellency would impart his wishes to me
frankly, as our Government could have no object
more at heart than to make him comfortable.   I
desired his Excellency to understand that secret
and indirect representations did not suit the station
of either of us; and I desired Mr. Ricketts to

inform him I would give his Excellency the opportunity this evening of unbosoming himself before the three secretaries, but without the presence of Major Baillie. The Nawab eagerly recapitulated to Mr. Ricketts all that he had said to Captain Gilbert; and when Mr. Ricketts was retiring, stopped him to whisper, "Cannot you get Major Baillie removed from Lucknow?" Before dinner I requested Major Baillie to stay with Lady Loudoun, while I took the Nawab and the three secretaries into another room. As soon as the door was shut the Nawab pulled out a paper and delivered it to Mr. Ricketts, saying that it was the second paper which he had promised, but which he had delayed sending. He said it contained a statement of all his wishes, except upon one point which yet interested him. Then he complained with great apparent sensibility of Major Baillie's preventing him from having the nobut (large drum) beat at sunrise, because the noise of it would disturb the Resident. He added that the beating the nobut was an article of dignity; and represented that he was lowered by not being allowed to do it. I said the point of the nobut should be settled directly

according to his wishes, and that his paper should
be considered without delay. We then repaired to
dinner.

November 1st.—I received the Delhi princes at
breakfast. They wore the high Tartar fur cap
instead of the turban. Their manners were without
polish, but respectful. After their departure, Mr.
Adam came to me, and communicated a most extraordinary message which he had just received.
Agha Meer, a favourite servant of his Excellency's,
came from the Nawab to say that his Excellency
had passed a sleepless night from reflection on what
had passed the evening before, and that his Excellency had in consequence sent him (Agha Meer)
to set the matter to rights. Agha Meer proceeded
to say that the Nawab Vizeer disavowed every
article in the paper delivered by him last night,
and desired it to be understood that he had been
over-persuaded by Mr. Clarke, who had written the
paper, to submit it as his own sentiment. The
paper was a long enumeration of grievances suffered
from Major Baillie. Mr. Adam asked Agha Meer
how it was possible for Mr. Clarke to have prevailed on the Nawab to take such a step in contra-

diction to his Excellency's own disposition.   Agha
Meer answered that the Nawab accounted for it
by Mr. Clarke's having asserted to him that the
Governor-General had a dislike to Major Baillie,
and would be gratified by his Excellency's furnishing a pretext for that gentleman's removal.   The
Nawab, according to Agha Meer, added that Mr.
Clarke, Captain Macleod, and Dr. Law had pressed
this opinion upon him before my arrival at Cawnpore.   This cannot be true.   Had the Nawab been
influenced to take this step against his own inclination, with the notion of doing what would have been
pleasing to me, he would have made the charge
roundly before the secretaries, so as to have afforded
me ground at Cawnpore to have dismissed Major
Baillie from his situation.   After my warning him
that indirect communications could not be attended
to by me, he would never have sought a conference
with Captain Gilbert as a mode of effecting my
purpose.   It is evident that the Nawab addressed
himself to Captain Gilbert because the latter had
married a cousin of Lady Loudoun's, who had come
out with her; his Excellency probably thinking that if he could gain upon Captain Gilbert's

feelings the representation would be made to me in a manner more likely to be effectual than through any formal channel.   Besides, he would have left the statements made by him to Mr. Ricketts to be worked upon by my judgment; and would not have closed his discourse by endeavouring to prevail on that gentleman personally to co-operate towards Major Baillie's removal.   I am glad that I have minuted these particulars, as they exhibit strikingly the little managements of an Asiatic Court.

November 2nd.—I sent for Mr. Clarke and Captain Macleod.   I told them that I judged it necessary to apprize them of what had been advanced by the Nawab Vizeer.   They persisted with the strongest asseverations in maintaining that the complaints against Major Baillie had originated with the Nawab himself; that he had repeatedly pressed the subject upon them; that his reiterated reference to them had led them to take part so far as to advise him to state his grievances to me personally; but that they had in no degree instigated the indisposition of the Nawab towards Major Baillie.   They both earnestly petitioned me to sit formally in the character of Governor-General in Council and receive their depositions on oath in the presence of the Nawab as to the falsity of his assertions. Mr. Clarke desired to swear that the paper in question was not of his writing, composition, or counselling. Both urged for permission to swear to the falsity of the assertion that either of them had ever told the Nawab Vizeer I was indisposed towards the Resident, a fact which they had never imagined. Though I felt it would be just to let them record this expurgatory affidavit, it was a proceeding incompatible with the delicacy to be observed with regard to a sovereign. Therefore I told them that I believed their declaration as firmly as I could do were it confirmed by oath; explaining to them the impossibility of my admitting any public proceeding which could so distinctly arraign the Nawab Vizeer of a wilful falsehood. I desired them to put upon paper a statement of what had occurred to them severally with his Excellency on this subject, and requested Mr. Ricketts to do the same. We had, in honour of the peace, a grand dinner, ball, and illumination at Constantia. The Nawab was present.

November 3rd.—I directed Mr. Ricketts, Mr. Adam, and Mr. Swinton to go from me to the Nawab Vizeer, with a solicitation that he will confidentially explain to them his real wishes, as I am so perplexed amid the strange circumstances which have occurred, that it is impossible for me to feel secure in my judgment of them. When they sent to request an audience, the Nawab, on pretence of indisposition, begged it might be put off till the morrow. The object of this delay is probably to consult on what steps he should take if they pressed him to an honest disclosure of his sentiments. Dr. Law came to me to profess, offering to verify it on oath, that there was not a word of truth in the Nawab's charge, that he (Dr. Law) had systematically endeavoured to inflame his Excellency against Major Baillie, and had insinuated that it would be pleasing to me to have accusations advanced against the Resident.

He told me that the Nawab had sent to reclaim not only an elephant, furnished to Dr. Law, as physician, but a one-horse chaise which the late Nawab had given to Mr. Law, and a portrait of himself, given by Saadut Ali to the doctor. Went in the afternoon to see the Hazree Baugh, a small country-house of the Nawab's, at the back of Dilk-oosha Park. It is very neat, standing in the midst of thick wood, on an elevation, with the front cleared so as to afford an extensive view of the cultivated plain on both sides of the Goomty.

November 4th.—Mr. Ricketts, Mr. Adam, and Mr. Swinton, waited on the Nawab Vizeer. He insisted that all his complaints had been made because Mr. Clarke, Captain Macleod, and Dr. Law had induced him to believe it would be a procedure by which he would recommend himself to my favour. He declared that so far from any estrangement with regard to Major Baillie, he felt warmly grateful for that gentleman's friendship, and desired nothing so much as his continuance at Lucknow.

The conference lasted nearly three hours, during which time the Nawab persevered in maintaining stoutly that Mr. Clarke, Captain Macleod, and Dr. Law, to whom his Excellency now added Monsieur De l'Etaing, had been long engaged in a conspiracy to ruin Major Baillie in his esteem; and though they had not effected their purpose, they had misled

him (the Nawab) to criminate the Resident. His
Excellency said that Dr. Law had never been his
physician, even during the lifetime of Saadut Ali;
he said that to satisfy his father he used to consult
Dr. Law when he was ill, but that he never followed Dr. Law's prescriptions, and always obtained
medicines privately from Mr. Wilson. This tallies
so ill with what passed in the phaeton that it cannot be true.   For some time past the Nawab had
been urged to appoint a minister for public affairs,
and another for finance; much inconvenience having
arisen from the want of these officers. The Nawab
had answered, that as his brother Shums-oo-Dowlah had been minister in the father's time, he (the
present Nawab) wished to appoint his son to the
honorary station.   He added that as his son was
still a child, it would be necessary to have a deputy
who would be the efficient minister; and he begged
me to choose the person for that purpose.   I
answered that I was highly sensible of the confidence reposed in me by the request, but that I could
not possibly interfere in an arrangement which was
so much to influence his comfort and welfare, further than to say that it would be inconvenient were

he to nominate a person whom the Resident represented as systematically adverse to the British Government, as was the case with Mehdy Ali Khan. Mr. Adam revived the subject this day, and the Nawab promised to settle the business. Before the gentlemen broke up the conference they, according to my instructions, adjured the Nawab in the most impressive manner to say whether any one had used my name, so as to occasion his Excellency's message by Agha Meer. He repeatedly declared that my name had not been so used. The question referred to a communication which Captain Macleod had made to me the day before yesterday. He said he had been secretly informed that Agha Meer, the morning after the conference at the Residency, had gone to the Nawab Vizeer and told him, with great apparent anxiety, that his Excellency had ruined himself with me; that I was furious at his having complained against Major Baillie; and that I even talked of removing him from the Musnud. It was stated that the Nawab, in his terror, asked what he could do to remedy the mischief, and was told that the only way was to disavow his paper, and impute his conduct to the machinations and suggestions of Mr. Clarke, Captain Macleod, and Dr. Law. The known devotion of Agha Meer to Major Baillie gave the story some verisimilitude.

November 5th.—We breakfasted with the Nawab. When that was over, I went to my palankeen, to return the visit of the Delhi princes. They live separately, and in very modest habitations. The visits went off very pleasantly for that kind of ceremony. I had been able to make for the princes an arrangement which freed them from some galling pecuniary difficulties, and they were very grateful. They gave atta, with their own hands, to my aides-de-camp—an attention which they had never shown in any instance before. They are tenacious in the extreme of their dignity, and the Nawab Vizeer cannot approach them without presenting a nuzzur. In the middle of the day I had a durbar at the Residency. It was much crowded. Several of the chiefs from the northern frontier claimed the right of presenting swords. Had I reserved to myself these tributes I should have a well-stocked armoury, but they are all delivered over to the Company. The Nawab Shudaroo-Dowlah, at above ninety years of age, had come more than one hundred miles to pay his compliments. I was informed of it before the durbar, and directed that he should not be let to stand in the crowd, but should be seated in an inner room. I went thither, sat beside him, and spoke to him with cheerful familiarity. The old man appeared touched with that kind of reception. I surprised agreeably one of the Affghan chiefs at the durbar. I had learned that his daughter had been betrothed to another chief, called Roostum Khan, but that the marriage had been delayed by Roostum Khan's having been arrested, by our Government, for secret machinations against it, and kept in confinement for the last six years. I told the Affghan chief that, as a compliment to his respectability and conduct, I would liberate Roostum Khan; only requesting that he (the Affghan) would counsel Roostum Khan as to his future behaviour. The man was wonderfully pleased. The exigencies of Government have rendered it unavoidable, in particular circumstances, to make state prisoners in this way. But this evil in the measure has not been sufficiently guarded against, that, as prisoners of this description are not within the cognizance of the magistrates, so as that Government shall be periodically reminded of them, the individuals are sometimes kept in custody after the considerations which required their detention no longer exist. We dined with the Nawab Vizeer. At the dessert a space was cleared opposite to the part of the table where the Nawab sat, between me and Lady Loudoun. A gang of buffoons were introduced, who began by imitating the cries of different animals; they then took off the singing and airs of the most distinguished nautch girls; but what seemed to give the greatest delight to the company was a man who represented a Bengalee, and got a prodigious number of slaps in the face for various acts of stupidity. The caricaturing the poor inhabitant of Bengal as a fool seemed to tickle the fancy of the Nawab Vizeer and all his kinsmen, no less than it excited the glee of all the up-country servants who were attending behind our chairs. When we rose from table, we went to the balcony, to see an illumination and fireworks. They were different from what had been displayed on the former night, and the whole was very splendid. Captain Macleod, Mr. Law, Mr. Clarke, and Monsieur De l'Etaing had been at the breakfast, in the morning, but were not invited to dinner.

November 6th.—We had divine service at Constantia, which was numerously attended by the ladies and officers from the cantonments. Captain Macleod asked for a private audience. He told me that he, Mr. Law, Mr. Clarke, and Monsieur De l'Etaing had received their formal dismission from the Nawab's service. He said that although the Nawab had forced upon him and Mr. Clarke, and possibly on Mr. Law, the task of listening to his Excellency's complaints against the Resident, he was satisfied the Nawab had never extended a similar confidence to Monsieur De l'Etaing. Adding that he thought it but justice towards a French *emigré* about to be exposed to great distress, to declare upon his honour that he had never spoken to Monsieur De l'Etaing on the subject, and that he was convinced Monsieur De l'Etaing was utterly unsuspicious of any such questions being in agitation. Captain Macleod proceeded to tell me,

that the Hakeem Mehdy Ali Khan had called upon
him, and desired that he (the Hakeem), might be
confronted by me with the Nawab Vizeer; in
which case he and two other persons who had been
present when Agha Meer addressed his master,
would testify that Agha Meer frightened the
Nawab into the recantation of the charges against
Major Baillie, by asserting my indignation at them
in the manner recorded by me on a former day. I
answered that I could well believe it; but that I
could not degrade the Vizeer by examining his
own attendants to disprove what he had chosen to
maintain perseveringly to the three public secretaries. I represented that it was not a case in
which I was to act as judge; for the employment
of Captain Macleod and the other gentlemen by
the Nawab was wholly a private transaction, and
it was altogether at his Excellency's pleasure to
say at any moment he had no further occasion for
their services. Relatively to our own Government,
I admitted their claim to be protected against any
imputation which might be unjustly advanced, on
which account, I said, I should put on record my conviction that there was some unaccountable inaccu-

racy in the Nawab's statement.   Major Baillie came
to me in the afternoon.   It was to apprize me that
a negotiation respecting Shums-oo-Dowlah had
been settled agreeably to my wishes; Shums-oo-
Dowlah, next brother to the Nawab Vizeer, had been
minister and commander of the troops during the
later years of Saadut Ali's life; there was an apprehension, I believe without the slightest foundation,
that he might make the hopeless attempt of dis-
puting the succession with his elder brother.   This
suspicion, and perhaps a dissatisfaction at the
greater degree of favour experienced from Saadut
Ali by Shums-oo-Dowlah, had deeply indisposed
the present Nawab against the latter.   His Excellency was therefore solicitous that Shums-oo-Dowlah should not reside at Lucknow, and the brother
was far from adverse to removal.   The Nawab
requested that I would constrain his brother to live
elsewhere.   I answered that if I interfered in the
affair it could only be on the terms of trying to
make the measure acceptable to Shums-oo-Dowlah;
towards which it would be necessary for his Excellency to grant an allowance so liberal as to counterbalance the advantages Shums-oo-Dowlah would

forego by quitting Lucknow. The arrangement this day notified to me is, that Shums-oo-Dowlah shall have a house and chace belonging to the Vizeer near Benares, with an allowance of two lacs of rupees yearly. This is certainly very handsome. I took occasion to express my surprise to Major Baillie that M. De l'Etaing who had been solicited by the Nawab to relinquish an advantageous office in the Company's stud, should be implicated in his Excellency's displeasure; stating that I could not conceive it likely for M. De l'Etaing to have had the slightest communication with the other gentlemen on the subject. Major Baillie answered he was persuaded M. De l'Etaing was not in the least involved in the business; "neither," said he, "does his Excellency expect it; but I believe the Nawab regrets the expense of having brought him hither, and is glad to take the opportunity of getting rid of him." The avowal is very curious: M. De l'Etaing has not been here six weeks; is a man of exemplary character and most polished manners; and is moreover highly qualified for superintending a stud, (the function he was to discharge here,) having held such an office under Louis XVI. in France. Luckily I can reinstate the poor man in the appointment he held in our stud. The Resident apprized me that the Nawab would the next morning send to me the arrangement of the ministry which was to be; his son as naib, or ostensible prime minister, Roy Dya Crishen, as peshcar or deputy, to be the real minister, and Agha Meer as dewan or minister of finance. The claims of Agha Meer, who had never in any discussions been adverted to as of a calibre for such advancement, surprised me much. He is a low man, who began as khidmutgar or footman to the Nawab, and waited behind his son's chair when the latter dined with me at Cawnpore. I did not express my wonder, only observing I could feel no right to interfere, unless the person contemplated by the Nawab were of known hostility to the British Government.

November 6th.—I went to shoot in the park of Dilkoosha, and brought home some partridges. On my return I was met by the painful news that Major-General Gillespie had been killed in an unsuccessful assault of the fortress of Kalunga. That he should have made so rash an attack is astonish-ing. The mischief which had occurred from in-considerate attempts to storm places by no means calculated to be carried in that manner, had made me insert as an article in the instructions to each of the generals commanding divisions, a special prohibition against that species of attack upon any works which should be of a quality to require artillery for their reduction. When Colonel Mawby was to be detached against Kalunga, Major-General Gillespie was directed by me to enforce upon Colonel Mawby's mind a strict attention to the above injunction. I received from Major-General Gillespie an answer, saying that he had impressed strongly on Colonel Mawby the caution dictated by me. Colonel Mawby, in consequence, on recon-noitering the place forebore to assault it, and re-ported to Major-General Gillespie that he meant to establish batteries against it, as he conceived it was impracticable to carry it by storm. The Major-General on this quitted his own column, repaired to the camp before Kalunga, and on examining the fortress resolved to assault it. The result was the only one that could be rationally expected.

The discredit to our arms, and the baneful influence which this reverse must have upon future operations, are light disadvantages in comparison to the loss of Major-General Gillespie. Whatsoever was the indiscretion of this last step, it cannot detract from the credit due to the many important services achieved by his heroic valour. His zeal, his energy, and his resources rendered him infinitely material for the conduct of operations in a country the features of which are so novel to officers unaccustomed to the plains of Hindostan. Genius like his would soon have fashioned others to a just conception of the system to be pursued in mountain warfare; and, deprived of him, I fear they will have to poke out their way amid many errors and oversights before they attain such experience as may give them due confidence in themselves. In the afternoon the Nawab Vizeer sent three rhinoceroses for our inspection. Two were females of middle growth. The third was quite young. They appeared tame and gentle.

November 8th.—This day, to my great surprise, Major Baillie informed me that the Nawab Vizeer had determined to make Agha Meer peshcar, and that Roy Dya Crishen was to be dewan. Of course Agha Meer is to be the effective minister for the guidance of all affairs. I could only say that, on principles already professed by me, I could have nothing to do with the Nawab's choice. It is impossible to see this arrangement and not to discover that the elevation of Agha Meer is the reward of the influence exerted by him over the Nawab Vizeer to produce those recantations which I have detailed. It is not my business to develope this intrigue; if the power which Major Baillie possesses over the Vizeer's mind, aided by the co-operation of Agha Meer, be exerted beneficially for the furtherance of public affairs, I can have no call to make objections. The interest of the individuals who have been immediately sacrificed in this juggle can be attended to by me hereafter. I believe that some sort of intimidation is the practice used with the Vizeer. He does not seem deficient in intellect, but he appears weak in nerve. I had observed that the bridge over the Goomty, though a handsome structure originally, was in a sad state of decay; and I had expressed my surprise that the Nawab Vizeer did not repair it before the damage should be beyond remedy. I was told that his Excellency had a firm persuasion that his repairing the bridge, or his suffering any of his family or servants to do it, would infallibly occasion his Excellency's death within the year. The edifice, therefore, equally an ornament and a convenience to the city, will perish through this strange misapprehension.

November 9th.—I received from the Nawab Vizeer a solicitation that I would be present next morning at a durbar, for the ceremony of investing his son and the subordinate ministers with the insignia of their offices. We dined at the Resident's to meet the Nawab Vizeer. On the occasion of my last dining at the palace I had praised highly some pillaw; I was told it had been dressed by the Nawab Cossim Ali (nephew of Saadut Ali), who sat opposite to me. He seemed very well pleased with my approbation of his cookery. In consequence, he sent to the Resident's two dishes of pillaw, and two of curry, on which he said he had exerted his utmost skill for the gratification of my palate. They were certainly excellent. Several kinds of pickles which he sent as a present to me the other day were no less admirable; but his taste may be exposed to some question from his making sweet conserves of turnips and candying radishes. Were he a wine drinker he would be a good counterpart of Falstaff. His bulk and his cheeriness of disposition remind me forcibly of the fat knight.

November 10th.—We breakfasted at the palace. When we rose from table, we proceeded to the durbar chamber, and took our seats. Shums-oo-Dowlah was introduced to take his formal leave. The Nawab Vizeer, without rising, put on his head a gaudy turban, after which the other parts of the khelaut, or dress of ceremony, were put upon him by the attendants. The Nawab's son was then introduced as naib. His Excellency insisted that he should receive from me the turban, and the other emblems of office. Among them I furnished him with a money-bag, an elephant iron, and a small pair of kettle-drums, which were to be suspended round his neck. They implied his title to use the nobut. Agha Meer and Roy Dya Crishen were then brought forward, and at the Nawab's entreaty I invested them also. The durbar being dissolved, we quitted the palace, and went to see the temporary tomb of Saadut Ali. A superb monument is about to be erected over his remains, but in the meantime, they are distinguished with the utmost magnificence. The body was interred in the middle of a garden; a temporary building of wood, elegant in form and richly japanned and gilt, is raised over the grave. Within the edifice a canopy of cloth of gold overhangs the sodded receptacle of the corpse. A large tiger of green glass (made in England) stood on each side of the frame that supported the canopy, and at the head were two large fishes of the same material. The fish is in India an emblem of sovereignty; attendants with chowries kept off the flies from the wreaths of fragrant flowers which decorated the pillars of the canopy; and several religious persons were employed in chanting verses of the Koran. When we came to our farewell dinner at the palace, the Vizeer thanked me in earnest terms for this attention to the memory of his father, saying that my kindness had soothed Saadut Ali's latter days.

This was a very curious expression; for my kindness to Saadut Ali had been only my rejection of a
system of coercion towards him, publicly urged
by Major Baillie, and so far acted upon before my
arrival in India, that Mr. Clarke asserted the Nawab
Vizeer to have described it as having broken his
father's heart. After dinner, at which Cossim Ali's
talents had been again felicitously displayed, the
buffoons were introduced; they went through their
former exhibition, Bengalee and all, without the
slightest variation; yet this uniformity did not seem
to diminish the interest which the native part of
the company took in the representation. After this
comedy a man played upon the bheem. The instrument has not much compass, or much melody,
to my ear. But the man sang to it in a manner
which made the whole of the performance very
pleasing. Lady Loudoun had made to the Nawab
Vizeer, to his son, and to a little brother whom his
Excellency had adopted as a son, some presents
curious to them, but of no intrinsic value. The
Nawab grounded on this an attempt to obtain her
acceptance of some magnificent jewels; but they
were sturdily declined. We adjourned to another

department where the formal leave-taking ensued. Wreaths of an uncommonly light silvery tinsel were put by the Vizeer over the neck of every European guest. We then embraced and separated. The young prime minister, from his frequent intercourse, had adopted great confidence in us, and he let us into a secret worth recording as characteristic of manners. The little brother of the Nawab's, mentioned above (a son of Saadut Ali by one of the women of the zenana), is quite a child, but is titular head of the judicial tribunal. He was sent with the Nawab's son, according to the etiquette, to the Resident's house to escort us to dinner. Lady Loudoun not being quite dressed, I made them sit down with me till she should be ready. Unfortunately the chief justice fell asleep. The Mentor who had accompanied him immediately roused him in spite of my entreaties, and took him out of the room. I concluded he had led the young dignitary into the verandah for the sake of air, as his somnolency might well be ascribed to the heat; and I was confirmed in my supposition when I shortly after saw the boy return and resume his chair with infinite gravity. The true state of the case, however, was confidentially unfolded to us by Nussor-oo-Deen, who told us his uncle had been conducted into another room and whipped for so gross a breach of ceremonious observances. Captain Gilbert, who had been one of the company at dinner, accompanied us to Constantia, and recounted to me an extraordinary phrase used by the Vizeer. The distribution of the wreaths produced an irregularity which left his Excellency more unobserved than was usually the case. He went up to Captain Gilbert, and taking the latter's hand pressed it to his heart; saying, "Notwithstanding all you have seen happen, my friendship shall never be divorced from you, as I hope I shall prove to you in happier times." The Captain represents him as having said this with a look of peculiar distress. As to all public matters, he had been put into a situation of comfort and dignity beyond his fondest hopes; therefore an expression which implied the present time to be not a happy one must have had allusion to his sense of prostration before some secret and inexplicable influence galling to his mind.

November 11th.—Marched from Constantia; forded the Goomty, and encamped just beyond the cantonment of the Lucknow subsidiary force.   In crossing the river the quick observation of an elephant manifested itself.   A camel was leading the way.   Finding the water deepen considerably, the camel, which does not swim, refused to go forward; and some contest took place between the animal and its rider from this obstinacy.   An elephant, which was following, was brought forward on the camel's being removed from the place; but neither coaxing or chastisement could induce him to proceed in the line where he had seen the camel struggling.   This must have arisen from his supposing that the bustle had been occasioned by the camel's getting its leg into some quicksand; for the elephant swims well, and willingly where there is sufficient water; and this elephant went on without solicitation when they had taken him some thirty or forty yards up the stream, though he had there to traverse a channel of greater depth.   The Persian Prince, Mirza Sooltaun Mahomed Suffuree, accompanied us to the camp.   He had asked leave to do this, that his being marked with such a favour might counteract the effects of his having been forced to descend from his seat on the Vizeer's musnud. I had before invited him to breakfast one morning, at Constantia, which I omitted to mention in its proper place.

November 12th.—Marched to Mohona, fourteen miles. The country fine and well cultivated.

November 13th.—The camp was in alarm all last night, from the quantity of thieves who had slidden into it. They are stark naked, so that creeping along the ground they are scarcely to be perceived ; and they are oiled all over, in order that it may be difficult to hold them, should they be seized. They crawl with infinite patience to a tent, slit the side with a knife, and then either enter or carry off whatsoever they may be able to reach with their arm, as circumstances tempt them. Many petty depredations were thus committed. Not one of the thieves was caught. But indeed the night was very dark, and it is only in such that these fellows make their attempts. Marched to Bacree, twelve miles. Divine service.

November 14th.—Last night a poor woman, who had put her little kettle on a fire where many others were cooking, returned for it when she thought the meat was dressed. Seeing some bustle round the fire, she feared to take her child into the crowd; therefore she sat it, with its back against a tree, not forty yards from the fire. She had not got half way to the fire, when the screams of her child made her run back, and she had the anguish of seeing a wolf carry it off. This was actually within the camp, and the sun had not been set above an hour. There must of course have been much cunning, as well as boldness, exhibited by the animal. Halted this day at Peernuggur, after a march of fourteen miles.

November 15th.—Marched to Seetapore, sixteen miles and a-half. We left the city of Kyrabad on our right, about a mile short of our encampment at this station. In the evening I reviewed the 1st battalion of the 15th Native Regiment, a fine corps.

November 16th.—Reached Mahowly, after a march of nearly sixteen miles. The tehsildar is nephew to Mehdy Ali Khan, who is entrusted with the superintendence of this district, though he resides at Lucknow. He met us as we approached the town, and wished to present me with some fine Persian greyhounds. I excused myself from accepting them, by pleading the number which the Nawab Vizeer had lent to me. He also produced, as a present to my son, a light carriage, drawn by two nylghaws. As the animals appeared remarkably fine, and had, more-over, silver ornaments about them, I conceived the present must be of intrinsic value, and therefore declined it. The nylghaws appeared very tractable, and drew the carriage with great rapidity. The bit to which the reins were attached was passed through the cartilage of the nostrils, as is done with all the draught oxen in this country.

November 17th.—After a march of fourteen miles and a-half we forded the Goomty, and encamped on its left bank.

November 14th to 18th.—Much thieving had continued in the camp. Last night, the servant of an officer was carrying a basket of linen to his master's tent, when a villain cut him across the arm with a large knife, and on the poor fellow dropping the basket, seized it, and carried it clear off, notwithstanding the alarm immediately given. We marched to Mahendy, eleven and a-half miles; a curious circumstance occurred. One of the gentlemen of my suite, who was riding at some distance on the flank of the line of march, was tempted to take a nearer view of a small town still farther from the road.   Perceiving, on his approach to it, a man, whose dress indicated him to be of the better class, he addressed himself to that person for the name of the place.   The man having satisfied the inquiry, said that the British had heavily disappointed the expectations of all the inhabitants in that district.   He said it had been understood that our Government meant to take possession of the territories of Oude, and that I was come up for the purpose; but that they had now been apprized of my having confirmed the Nawab's authority.   The English gentleman (who spoke the Hindostanee language perfectly) asked him, with some surprise, whether it had indeed been the wish of the people to see their country transferred to a foreign rule.   The man laughed, and answered, "To be sure it was our wish.   Can you think us such fools as not to desire to have our estates, and the earnings of our industry secure?   We must always be exposed to the cupidity of a native sovereign; but we know that the British, either from a spirit of justice, or from policy, always leave individuals in the enjoyment of their property."

November 19th.—After a march of twelve and a-half miles, we halted at Powain, the first town in the Company's territories. The Vizeer's country from Lucknow hither is rich in point of soil, and is in general well cultivated; indeed, I should rate it higher in both respects than some of ours to the south-east. On this frontier, however, there was a most striking difference between the state of the lands, and the apparent comfort of the inhabitants in the two districts decidedly in favour of ours.

November 20th.—Halted at Powain, and had divine service.

November 21st.—Marched something above fourteen miles to Bimrowlee. A wolf crossed the line of march without showing any alarm, and without any attempt to disquiet it being made by the natives close to where it passed. It went into a field of sugar-canes, whence it could not have been driven by the elephants without their doing great mischief to the crop.

November 22nd.—Marched thirteen miles to Bissulpore.

November 23rd.—Reached Gujnerah. It should have been mentioned that we re-crossed the Goomty on the 18th, before we reached Mahowdy.

November 24th.—Reached Bareilly after a march of fifteen miles. On the approach to this, as well as to every other considerable town I have seen in this country, one is struck with the number of public buildings gone to complete ruin. It has been occasioned by oppressive Governments which took no care of edifices productive of no revenue, and left no means to individuals who might have been disposed to keep up what they probably considered as ornaments in their country.

November 25th.—I had a levee for the European gentlemen: Sir Edward Colebrooke, commissioner; Mr. Hawkins, judge of circuit; Mr. Dumbleton, magistrate; Mr. Low, collector; Mr. Moore, secretary to the commissioners, were the principal civilians. In the afternoon I went to look at the city. The Jumma Musjeed, a mosque as we term it, is the only building worthy notice. It has been a handsome edifice, but is falling fast to decay. The minarets have been rather elegantly ornamented with enamelled tiles. They have dropped out in many places, so as that the pattern of the roof is spoiled. The position of the building is bad, being in a narrow street. We were told this was owing to the intolerance of the Moslems, who would not be satisfied with raising their mus-jeed anywhere but on the site of the chief Hindoo temple.

November 26th.—I had a durbar for the principal inhabitants of the town. On inquiring about their last harvest, I learned that the price of gram in Bareilly was less than the value of an English shilling for an English quarter. It was purchase-able by the pound at that rate. Gram is a species of tare; universally preferred here to oats for horses, and forming no bad food for man when dressed with ghee or curry-powder.

November 27th.—We had divine service, nume-rously attended by the civilians, officers, and wives of both classes. Two years had elapsed since they had last the opportunity of attending public worship. The extent of this country, and the remoteness of stations from each other, escape the comprehension of people at home, so that the insufficiency of the present establishment of chaplains is never suspected. In the afternoon we drove about the environs of the city. It was lamentable to see the handsome tomb of Hafiz Rukmut already in a state of progressive dilapidation. He was a kinsman to Fyzoolla Khan, the Rohilla chief, and general of his armies. The gallant and elevated character of the man deserved that his monument should be more durable.

November 28th.—Marched to Futtehgunje, crossing the Dojoora by a bridge, and encamped on the ground upon which the Rohilla army formed before it advanced to attack Sir Robert Abercromby. There is a small elevation of ground in this part, which commands the portion of the plain where Sir Robert's army was encamped. This advantageous spot had been rather unaccountably neglected, and the enemy judiciously occupied it with their cannon. The benefit to be derived from this position for their artillery was sacrificed to a premature charge of cavalry, which, though at first it succeeded so far as to threaten total defeat, was utterly repulsed.

When the guns were no longer covered by the enemy's cavalry, they were speedily taken by our infantry, and the Rohillas fled in confusion. On the little hill, a monument is erected to the memory of those officers of ours who fell on the occasion and were buried there; and close to it is a tomb after the Mahomedan fashion, over the bodies of Fyzoolla Khan and such of his officers as were slain in the conflict.

November 29th.—Crossed by a ford the Dojoora river, and encamped at Meergunje.

November 30th.—Reached Kumora Dumora, in the State of the Nawab of Rampore.

December 1st.—As this chief of the Rohillas had come to visit me when I was at Bareilly, I thought it would not be civil to pass within four or five miles of his residence without calling upon him; I, therefore, this day left the column to pursue its course, and I turned off for the city of Rampore. The Nawab, with a very large retinue of elephants and horsemen, met us about three miles from the city. After having paid his compliments, he begged that we would advance gently, so that he might get back to his palace before our arrival, and be in readiness to receive me. The land close to Rampore appears strangely neglected, though other parts of the territory are in high cultivation. A tall hedge of the thorny bamboo surrounds the town, and forms an impenetrable fence. The streets are narrow and tortuous beyond the usual amount of that defect in Indian towns, and the houses are very poor. The palace has no show, and seems much neglected. Having got through the double gateway, I found the Nawab waiting afoot in the court. He obliged me to walk upon fine silk across that court; and, when we reached the next, pieces of gold or silver brocade were spread till I reached a splendid chair prepared for me in the hall of audience. This magnificence contrasted singularly with the want of other decorations in the apartments. When I was seated, his kinsmen and principal officers were presented: the articles were very valuable, particularly some jewels destined for Lady Loudoun. There were two swords, by much the handsomest and of the best taste I have seen in India. When I perseveringly declined the present, on the ground that I had accepted the trays which he offered at Bareilly, and that Lady Loudoun never took anything of intrinsic value, he pressed the swords upon me most importunately, appealing to his minister whether they had not been mounted on purpose for me; but as the hilts and scabbards of both were set with precious stones I was inflexible in declining them. I said that to show him my refusal did not proceed from any motive but my having already accepted a present from him (which I could not tell him would be sold on account of the Company), I would take one article; and I fixed upon a pair of warm stockings from Cashmere. I am glad I made that choice, for it gave me the opportunity of observing that they are made of a sort of felt. The material looks like the South American vicuña's wool. Probably it is from some kind of goat. On taking leave of the Nawab, he begged very hard that he might be allowed to send to my tent the chair on which I had been sitting; as likewise 1000 rupees for my servants. Here was a new contest, which was at last compromised by my allowing the servants to receive the usual boon of the brocades and silks on which I had stepped. Fording the Cossilah River, which we skirted immediately after coming out of the city, I reached my camp on its western bank. We were now in the Zillah of Moradabad; and the gentlemen of that station met me here. Mr. Old-ham, the magistrate; Mr. Chalmer, the registrar; Mr. Batson, the collector; Mr. Rutherford, Com-missary-General's department; Mr. Ker, appointed one of the judges of the Suddur, Dewan Dowlut, also came; and Mr. Colin Shakespear, collector of Meerut, likewise joined us. Sir E. Colebrooke, Mr. Hawkins, and Mr. Moore had accompanied us from Bareilly.

December 2nd.—We reached Moradabad, fording the Ramgunga close under the town. We had previously crossed another branch of the river about two miles off. In the rainy season, the whole interjacent tract is a sheet of water; now it is covered with a most promising growth of wheat. On approaching the branch close to the city, we were much struck with the appearance of three round towers, one of them very perfect, in the middle of the stream. Various conjectures were entertained as to the use of these singular buildings, till the solution was afforded us by the magistrate. These were the linings of wells, and when the river,

gradually wearing the elevated bank on which
Moradabad is situated, effected its present channel,
those buildings from their shape and depth of
foundation remained undestroyed, though all the
edifices which the water could sap had disappeared.
The top of one of these apparent towers was now
just on a level with the top of the bank about one
hundred and fifty yards from it, all the earth that
had formerly existed between having been washed
away. In moving towards our camp, which was
beyond the town, we had to observe the peculiar
structure of the latter. It was in four divisions;
each walled with its own gates, and separated by a
space which reminded me of the road from Kingston
to Hampton Court, between Bushey and Hampton
Court Parks. We encamped in a beautiful grove
of mango-trees, from which we looked over a vast
unbroken extent of plain, exhibiting quite an oceanic
appearance.

December 4th.—Heavy rain fell in the night. Its
consequences were very gratifying. The air though
dry had been to a certain degree hazy. It now
became perfectly clear, and gave us a most interesting view of the summits of the Himalaya Mountains

towering above the elevated ridges of Camaron. The latter, consisting of three, and in some places four ranges, rising one above the other, would be elsewhere considered as very high; but they shrink to insignificance in comparison with the splendid peaks behind them. The Himalaya Mountains, separating Tartary from Hindostan, are probably the highest in the world. There is something no less picturesque than sublime in the forms of those regions of eternal snow when seen from this position. We had divine service.

December 5th.—We went out this morning to have a view of the snowy mountains from different points. It is a spectacle so sublime that the eye never tires of it. The servants whom we had brought with us from Calcutta could not be made to comprehend the nature of what they gazed at. They had seen iced cream, and they could not separate the notion of art from the snow when an attempt was made to explain what they looked at by referring to their acquaintance with ice. When one thought them convinced, they uniformly returned to the question how it was done. A Bengal draftsman who accompanied us was directed to make a coloured sketch of the scenery, and he resented as an imposition on his understanding an endeavour to persuade him that the white pinnacles were not clouds.   In the middle of the day I had a durbar to receive some Rohilla chiefs, some vakeels, and a good many of the principal inhabitants of Moradabad.   They having been introduced at a durbar stamps gentility with these people as much as the being presented at Court does with us; therefore the holding of a durbar for them is felt as a particular compliment, and surely it is incumbent that their feelings should be consulted when the gratification of them exacts nothing but an immaterial degree of trouble.   Regret that I did not minute in the proper places the visits of some chiefs whose names I may wish to remember makes me revert to those days in order to insert part of the list here.   At Bissulpore I received the Nawab of Furruckabad, Shoohud Jung, and his brother, Nusrut Jung. They are both young boys, of amiable countenance and good address.   Their guardian, Moonshy Khoda Buksh, was with them.   He said that the life of a man at his age was precarious, on which account he wished I would let the young Nawab offer a petition. The latter then advanced, said he could have no security but in the British protection, and begged I would consider him as a child of mine. I assured him of the vigilance of Government over his welfare. His kinsmen, Ashruf Ali Khan, Imdaud Hoseyn Khan, Himmut Ali Khan, Imaum-oo-Deen, Boo Ali Khan, Wullee Oolla Khan Bahadur, and Sheer Ali Khan, were then presented.

These Patans are stout, frank-looking men, with much martial air. They did not maintain the cold reserve usual among the Mussulmans, but cheerfully expressed their satisfaction at being received with an appearance of kindness. Saadi Ali Khan and Hukeem Gholam Ali Hoseyn Khan, deputed to compliment me by the Nawab of Rampore, were also introduced. At Bareilly I received Ahmud Ali Khan, Nawab of Rampore. He was accompanied by his two uncles, Cossim Ali Khan and Kurreem Oolla Khan; also by the following kinsmen, Neyaz Ali Khan, Saadut Ali Khan, Mozuffur Ali Khan, Jaafer Ali Khan, Inayut Ali Khan, Iband Oolla Khan, Abdul Ali Khan, Ahmud Yar Kahn, Fulsuh Oolla Khan, Ahmed

Oolla Khan, Keramez Oolla Khan, and Ali Ahmed Khan.

This was on the 24th of November. On the following day I received a set, who appeared to me to have been not desirous of mixing with the others. They were the sons of Hafiz Rukmut Khan; viz., Nawab Mahomed Yar Khan, Nawab Ali Yar Khan, Nawab Omer Khan, and Nawab Mustajaul Khan, with a number of young men, their sons. All these Rohillas were well dressed, and were good-looking men in general; but they did not show the animated confidence of the Patans. Their retinue, however, was composed of fine men well-appointed. Many inhabitants of the city of Bareilly attended, as did likewise the vakeel of Nawab Bumboo Khan, with Deasan Jowahir Laul, Fonjdar Motee Ran, and Chowdry Dya Sunkur, vakeels from the Rajah of Bhurtpore. This present day I have received Nawab Ayoob Khan, grandson of Hafiz Rukmut, with two of his cousins, Rajah Laul Sing, representative of the family expelled from the Government of Kemaoon by the Gorkhas; and many principal people of this vicinity. In addition to these, there were vakeels from Surfuranze Muhul, mother of the Nawab of Furruckabad, from Dya Ram, of Hattrass, from Bughwunt Sing, from Bukht Sing, near Adjeghur, and a fresh one from Bumboo Khan. This latter personage is son of the late Zabita Khan, and brother to the Gholam Khadir who put out the eyes of the King of Delhi.

December 6th. — Continued at Moradabad. Nothing particular occurred.

December 7th.—The slow progress of a deputation from the King of Delhi detained us inconveniently here. It would be ungracious to give such individuals as are sent on this occasion the additional trouble of following me further. Besides, a deputation from the King is so extraordinary a circumstance, that it is well it should be witnessed by the inhabitants of a large city. We went through the different parts of the town. It has been handsome without magnificence. It had fallen into a state of sad decay and desertion; but under our Government, the population and opulence of the city are retrieving themselves rapidly. The people looked comfortable, and were highly respectful.

December 8th.—We went to the Cutcherry, or Sessions House, that from the flat roof of that elevated building we might see the first rays of the rising sun strike on the summits of the snow ridge. The sight was truly grand. The snow, illuminated by the beams, looked exquisitely brilliant. There was an odd sensation in contemplating a spot on the globe where the foot of man had never trod, or was ever likely to be planted. This immense barrier would seem sufficient to limit the concerns of India; yet at this moment I am speculating on the trade which may be carried on beyond it, should the present war with the Gorkhas leave us in possession of Kemaoon. From that province there are valleys between the hills which afford passage of not much difficulty, and greatly frequented, into Tartary. The holding of Kemaoon would give to us the exclusive purchase of the shawl wool, to be paid for in cutlery, broad-cloth, and grain.

December 9th.—Heavy rain.

December 10th.—The rain, which had continued through the morning, cleared up in the afternoon. The superstition of the people gives me all the credit for this rain, which is most useful to them. "Faire la pluie et le beau temps" is not metaphorically applied by them to the Governor-General.

The deputation from Delhi arrived this day, and encamped close to us.

December 11th.—I this day received the deputation. It consisted of the following persons:— Nawab Azeem-oo-Dowlah Mohummed Meer Khan, Dewan of the Queen Momtaj Muhul, and reckoned the ablest of the council; Nawab Shums-oo-Dowlah Bukhshee Mirza Mahmood Khan, Commander of the Household Cavalry; Nawab Shahbauze Khan Chugta, Vakeel of the King with the Resident; Nawab Coolb-oo-Dowlah Kootb-oo-Deen Khan, of high family, and one of the principal courtiers; Mirza Kanjeh Kuddur Nant, assistant to the Nazr of the King; Nawab Rooku-oo-Dowlah Roshun-oo-Deen Khan, late Commander of the Cavalry, and now Head Physician; Dubeer-oo-Dowlah Khanjeh Fursud-oo-Deen Ahmed, Aumeen of the Royal Household; and Rajah Juc Seekh Roy, assistant to the Aumeen. The above are principal officers of state, and out of compliment to them, or out of curiosity, a number of the most distinguished courtiers had spontaneously joined the deputation. They were as follows:—Nawab Mobarek-oo-Dowlah; Mirza Hassan-oo-Deen Hyder Khan, a person of distinguished family; Meer Mohammud Khan, a confidential officer of the Queen's; Ameer-oo-Dowlah Nuwazish Khan, nephew of the Prime Minister; Nawab Pururish Khan Meer Bonhain Ali Khan, brother of the last; Meer Zulfar Ali Khan, son of the preceding; Meer Hyder Ali Khan, an officer of Queen Momtaj Muhul's household; Cooar Narrain Doss, son of Rajah Sree Mull, and nephew of Rajah Seikh Roy; Rao Shedhoo Ram, Peshcar (or deputy) of the High Treasurer; Hakeem Hassan Buksh Khan, and Hukeem Sadi Ali Khan, Physicians to the King; Hafez Abool Mowee Yad Khan, an individual of marked station.

They were all splendid in retinue and dress; and it was impossible not to observe in their air and manners the tone of highly-polished society. They presented their nuzzurs separately, and then were requested to take chairs. When they were seated, the head of the deputation made me a compliment on the part of the king, to which the due answer was made. Conversation succeeded. Then Azeem-oo-Dowlah requested that he might deliver to one of my attendants for me a sword which the king entreated me to accept. His Majesty desired that I should be told that it was the sword which Aurungzebe used to wear, and that he should have thought it sinful to let it go out of his family to any person but to me. This mode of presenting the sword, of putting it into the care of an attendant, was a delicacy of attention, lest the delivering it directly to myself should imply that the king sent me a weapon to be used in his defence.

The compliment was altogether well imagined, as the sword is to be prized from the circumstance of its having belonged to Aurungzebe, while it had no intrinsic value. It is a simple tulwar, the hilt of which is only of silver and brass. From two Persian lines engraven on the blade, and which have all the air of antiquity, I have no doubt but that the sword really was Aurungzebe's. I invested every member of the deputation with a rich khelaut. Many natives unconnected with the deputation were present. Among them were these :—Rajah Unroodh Sing, of Bullunghur;

Coom Ranj Sing, his grand-uncle, and adminis-
trator of the territory during the Rajah's minority;
Coom Bughwunt Sing, the Rajah's uncle; Nawab
Fyze Mohammud Khan, son of the late Nejabut
Ali Khan, chief of Kanoor, &c.; Nawab Ahmed
Buksh Khan, of Feerozpoor; Mirza Futteh Oola
Beg Khan, his nephew; Nawab Fyz Oolla Beg
Khan, of Husseea; his sons, Gholam Nukshbund
Khan, and Gholam Morteza Khan; Nawab Mor-
tesa Khan, of Peloul; his sons, Mustapha Khan
and Wullee Mohammed Khan; Bukshee Bhowany
Sunkur, chief of Nujufghur; his sons Jehangeer
Chund and Jyesookle Roy, with his son-in-law,
Kishen Chund; Rao Kesree Sing, claimant of the
Gudda of Rewarry; Nawab Abbas Kooli Khan,
nephew of the late Vizier of Cabul; Rajah Keywul
Nyne, vakeel from Scindiah; Nawab Urfaa-oo-
Dowlah, vakeel of the Rana Keerut Sing; Roy
Dala Kam, vakeel of the Rajah of Jodepore;
Iumeent Sing, vakeel from Runjeet Sing to the
Resident at Delhi; Lala Bhool Chund, vakeel of
the Rajah of Keytuh; Ruttun Chund, vakeel of
the Rajah of Banswara; Rajah Puddun Sing,
vakeel of the Rao Rajah (of Macherry), and Urgun

Sing, vakeel of Juswunt Sing, the Sikh chief of Nubba.

These apparently unmeaning lists are not useless to record; for individuals in this country start up so suddenly to power and celebrity, that it is interesting to preserve some clue by which one's memory may be aided in retracing the appearance of the person. The Patan chiefs present on this occasion were a fine martial set of men, and their attendants were as sturdy-looking fellows as I have ever seen.

The ceremony of this day is not of an indifferent nature. After the durbar had broken up, Dr. Hare (my physician) got into conversation with some of the Patan chieftains who were walking about the camp, his fluent command of the language enabling him to address them without difficulty. Though nothing appeared to lead to the remark, they told him they had been talking about what they had just seen, adding that they were very glad to have witnessed it. "We know now," said they, "to whom we belong. We thought the British were only appointed to take care of this territory for a time; but we now see that the

British Government is our sovereign." This impression of the legitimacy and permanence of our rule is far from immaterial. Divine service in the afternoon.

December 12th.—I gave to the deputation their audience of leave; and we parted in a very good-humoured manner.

December 13th.—Quitted Moradabad, recrossing the Ramgunga at the part of the town opposite from that at which we had intended, and steering our course towards the mountains. A vast tract of barren sand shows the extent to which the Ramgunga in the rainy season overflows the country, and proves that no fertilizing mud is suspended in its water. Indeed, we had here noticed with gratification a clear stream. All the rivers which one sees in the lower country are turbid. Halted at Bojipore.

December 14th.—Reached Balawala. Large herds of antelopes were seen on both sides of the line of march, but they appeared very shy. We had four or five flights of hawks after paddy-birds (a species of small heron), which were not amiss. The paddy-bird is very skilful at dodging in the air. Bumboo Khan visited me here. He is a son of Zabeta Khan, and had the province of Hurreanah conferred on him for his services with Lord Lake. Unable to maintain himself there against the predatory hordes, he solicited permission to exchange that Jagheer for a pension, upon which he now lives in much state in this neighbourhood. His figure must formerly have been fine; but he now appears enervated and stupified, probably with the use of opium.

December 15th.—Halted at Kasheepoor, rather three separate hamlets than a town, though it is a considerable mart in the commerce with the hills. We were now so near them that it was requisite to keep cavalry patrols going all night to the edge of the forest, as a security against attempts from the Gorkhas.

December 16th.—A little before the hour at which the march of the camp was to begin, the sporting party mounted the elephants, and we advanced towards the hills in search of a tiger of which we had notice. The ground over which we passed was a plain destitute of trees, which runs like a bay into the forest nearly to the foot of the hills. We did not see a tiger, though we hit upon the footing of two. We followed the tracks above a couple of hours, and could perceive by the prints that the animals must be but a very short way before us. The tall wiry grass with which the plain was covered would conceal a tiger from our view at a very little distance, while it was so thinned as to afford him no obstruction in getting away. We sacrificed our sport at deer, which were plenty, in this unavailing pursuit. Giving up at length, we struck through the skirts of the forest for about seven miles to reach our new encampment at Jusspore. We saw a large lynx in our way, as also one of a smaller sort. Both of these escaped, but we killed some deer and pea-fowl. We had been so near to the hills as to see distinctly the passes, which did not appear to me so difficult as they are represented.

December 17th.—We reached Affzulghur.

December 20th.—Marched to Nujeenah. Our course was now parallel to the hills. The scenery was very fine, though the peaks of the snow-ridge are not seen so well here as at Moradabad. We are too close under the nearer ranges.

December 21st.—We, the sporting party, quitted the line of march to penetrate a little into the forest, in hopes of finding plenty of game. In that respect we were disappointed, unless as to the smaller sorts. We got a quantity of hares and partridges, with three or four floricans, also some jungle-fowls. But we saw no deer or bears, which we had been taught to expect. There were monkeys in great numbers. At them, however, we did not shoot. We got about the middle of the day to our camp, having been strangely delayed in the forest by ravines, extraordinarily difficult to pass. That feature made a marked difference between this part of the forest and that which was seen near Kasheepoor. In other respects they are similar. The trees of bad kind, and bad of the kind, standing wide from each other, with a brushwood easily traversed in every direction. Our camp was between the town of Nujeebabad and the deserted fort of Putturghur. The latter is a very large square, within which Nujeeb Khan, who built it, meant to establish a city, to be peopled from the existing town of Nujeebabad. By his judicious encouragement of commerce, he had made this spot a considerable emporium of trade; and he wished to give it security. The irruptions of Nadir Shah, and the consequent troubles of Hindostan, destroyed his speculations. The fort was besieged by Nadir Shah, who soon called off his troops to more important objects. It strikes me that this place might be repaired at little expense, and might be made an excellent station for a light corps.

December 22nd.—We went through the town of Nujeebabad. It retained marks of having been once the seat of activity and enterprise. Our halting place was Asophgurh. There is a fort here with handsome gateways and in good condition. But no human creature lives here. After the fortress had been built and a town established, the spot proved so dreadfully unhealthy that it was of necessity abandoned. We did not like the resting here even for a few hours. But the quantity of water required for our numerous train often obliges us to take up ground in other respects objectionable. Travellers, moreover, dislike this place, from the extraordinary vigilance they are forced to observe in driving away the wild elephants, who otherwise seduce the tamed ones to go off with them.

December 23rd.—We started before dawn to get some shooting, while our camp should be passing the Ganges. The whole country round Asophgurh is a series of reed beds, divided by patches of higher soil, on which amid trees and long grass, one expects to find game of the larger class. In the reed-beds we found numberless places where it was evident wild elephants had been just lying; and it is extraordinary how dexterously they must have managed to have got off without being perceived. We did not see one the whole day. I have shot a woodcock, of a kind new to me, and I think not mentioned by ornithologists. The English in these parts call it the solitary snipe, from having heard of such a bird in Europe. But this kind differs wholly from the snipe distinguished by that name, except as to size, in which they are nearly alike. The legs are green. Its flight is exactly that of a woodcock. I understand it is always found in the reed-beds adjoining to woods. I shot a hind of the large red deer species with one of a smaller kind, and a quantity of inferior game.

We did not, however, find any beasts of prey; indeed we had good proof that (although you may stumble upon one by chance in the midst of your shooting) there is no reckoning upon finding these beasts but by proceeding silently; and sacrificing other objects to them. We this day repeatedly came on the tracks of tigers, which were obviously making off from us, in consequence of our repeated firing. I remarked this day, as I had done yesterday, how singularly the line of the forest is defined on the plain. It appears as if it had been planted regularly. No dotting trees or thickets connect it with the open ground. When our sport was over, we crossed the Ganges. It is divided by a large island into two streams, each of them magnificent. The water is deep, brilliantly limpid, and the current strong; with a bottom of large round pebbles, which made the footing apparently unsteady for our elephants. The care they take in balancing themselves is admirable. We found our camp pitched at Boajpore, a little village about a mile from the ford.

December 24th.—The spot on which our camp stood was devoid of feature, and the first portion

of this day's march was through a dull, ill-cul-
tivated flat. As we approached Hurdwar, however, groves and flourishing hamlets presented
themselves. It is very remarkable that there is
not any alteration of ground to indicate approxi-
mation to the mountains. In all other countries
which now occur to my recollection, minor hills
rise in succession before you come to a principal
range. Here, the mountains start abruptly from
the plain, and with such steep acclivity, that they
are to be ascended at particular passes. The village, or rather open town of Kunkul, about two
miles from Hurdwar, was the first testimony to
the expenditure of riches in this neighbourhood.
A number of handsome buildings bespeak the
opulence of the owners. It was gratifying to learn
that almost all of them had been erected since the
territory came under our dominion; the security
for enjoyment of them being the inducement to
this application of money. Many of the mansions
were elegant in architecture, but there was scarcely
one which was not disfigured by wretched paintings
of tigers or elephants, or with mythological representations of just such a rate of art as one would

see on the most paltry pot-house in England.
Hurdwar lies so much behind an elbow of the hill
that one sees little of it in approaching by this
road.   A view of the town, however, is easily dispensed with, amid the other beauties which present
themselves, on your emerging from some of the
tufts of mango-trees and gaining a sudden sight of
the valley through which the Ganges runs between
the hills.   The scenery is glorious.   The nearer
mountains are abrupt, woody, and various in form.
The remoter ranges look austere and imposing.
The river, divided at this season into several
channels, has nothing immediately striking; but
it is impossible not to perceive at once how vast a
bed it fills in the time of its plenitude, and the
mind recognises the worshipped stream.   Our own
tents were pitched on a narrow flat between the
hill and the nearest channel of the river, just at
the entrance of the town.   Other parts of the camp
were on a ledge of the hill or on an island, beyond
the fordable channel.   We went to see the famous
bathing ghaut.   The building is a large mass of
freestone, far from inelegant in notion, but squeezed
together from the narrowness of the space between

the mountain and the water. We ascended by a
very broad and high flight of steps to the flat roof
of a sort of tower, whence there is a fine view of the
river. This was not the season for the periodical
bathing of devotees, who at those periods flock
thither in such numbers that the concourse is estimated at above one million. We saw nothing
but some of the charitable residents feeding the
sanctified fish which, secure from injury, came in
large shoals, and individually great in size, to the
steps to receive their accustomed meal. Our followers, indeed, soon hastened to wash away all sins
in the sacred water, and underwent the shaving,
for which the Brahmins exact a heavy remuneration.
We also saw the sale of Ganges water in very light,
thin green bottles made here for the purpose. The
Brahmins vend this consecrated lymph very dear to
pilgrims, who are coming in uninterrupted succession from all parts of India to procure it, in order
to wash with it the representatives of their deities.
We were well acquainted with these migratory
parties, of whom we had passed in our road multitudes either advancing or returning. They are not
more distinguishable by the particular basket which

they carry at each end of a pliant bamboo than by the singular salutation with which they greet all who approach them. A round and vehement intona-tion of Bum Bahaudur addressed to all travellers is infinitely meritorious in their conception; and when one happens to meet a string of these good folks the peal has a very whimsical effect. One perceives the policy of the Brahmins in enjoining these pilgri-mages to the extremities of the territory as a duty imperative on every one who professes to fulfil the articles of his faith.   Uniformity of superstition is kept up by this intercourse between the remotest quarters; and the devotee receives at these distant points of his veneration a revived impression which rivets the influence of his own local Brahmin over him.

December 25th.—We had divine service and communion.   There was something singular in keeping our Christmas-day in the very head quar-ters of the Brahminical mysteries.   I ordered com-fortable dinners for the bodyguard, as well as for our servants, and I sent a thousand rupees to the Brahmins at the ghauts.   In the afternoon we visited the Chund Puhur (or Moon Mountain), on the other side of the river; a small muth, or temple, is visible on the top of it from Hurdwar; but the eye is still more attracted by an English flag, which an old priestess hoists in token of the protection she receives from the Government. After she had alone officiated at the altar for several years, some of the fakeers learnt that she got a good deal of money from those who visited the spot, either out of curiosity or devotion, and they forcibly deposed her. She complained to the British magistrate of the district, who justly considered her right of preoccupation as entitling her to the advantages of the situation, and replaced her in it, furnishing her with a written order to all the native police-officers to see her redressed in case of future intrusion. We passed four or five minor streams of the river on our elephants. The further and main channel was not fordable. We crossed it in a boat so frail and leaky that I was not without my apprehensions it might have gone to pieces in the middle of the river. The ascent begins immediately from the eastern bank. It is a very steep and narrow path, and the gaining the summit is really a laborious effort. The view did not so well repay the toil as I expected. The course of the river in the plain afforded no picture. To the eastward, a higher range of hill rose close upon you, and barred all prospect. Hurdwar was brought too much beneath us, and rendered too indistinct by our height to display much feature; and haze obscured the valley towards the snowy mountains, now hidden from us through our proximity to the intervening ranges. I gave the old woman a present, and added a confirmation of her title to hold the station of officiating priestess. She has a daughter whom she destines to be her successor.

December 26th.—We set out very early in the morning for an excursion up the valley, meaning to make it a shooting party as well as a reconnoitring expedition. Though we had not heard of any tigers, we were in hopes of finding some, from one having been killed in an island of the Ganges by a party of our gentlemen on the 24th. They had quitted the line of march to beat an island they had remarked as affording strong cover. Immediately on entering it, they roused a tiger, which attacked them directly. Some of their elephants not being steady, the party were thrown into confusion by the charge, and three of the elephants were much torn by the tiger before he was killed. He was uncommonly large and strong. A gentleman who was mounted on a bulky elephant, assured me that it was nearly pulled to the ground by the tiger, who had fixed his claws in the elephant's ears. The road from Hurdwar up the valley runs along the face of the hill, and soon becomes so narrow and precipitous that, although an elephant would probably pass it with perfect security, the feeling of the rider would not be quite comfortable. We therefore undertook to ford the first channel of the river in order to recross it when we should have got so high as where a cross valley runs at the back of the hill. To effect this, we advanced nearly to the bathing ghauts, and then went into the river by descending some stone steps. The dexterity of the elephants in going down these stairs was really curious. They went slanting, so as to gain sufficient breadth on the step for their foot, and though they proceeded with great caution, trying, as it were, whether their balance was firm, they showed no hesitation. Having got to the end of the island,

or rather bare bed of large pebbles, which we had
first gained, we had to traverse a stream that
divided us from another island. This passage was
rendered difficult by the great force of the water
which rushed over a natural mound or weir of
stones. This embarrassment the elephants encountered and surmounted with great confidence,
though the slipperiness of the large stones under
water was evidently very troublesome to them.

From this second island we soon regained the
main, and found ourselves amid very picturesque
scenery. Our progress was chiefly through a
forest, the trees standing wide from each other,
and with little underwood; amid which every now
and then there was a cultivated spot with five or
six peasants' huts grouped together. From these
openings we had varied views of the woody hills
around, the more striking to us from our long subjection to the uniformity of the flat country. We
advanced thus up the western bank of the river for
three or four miles. Several deer and peafowl
were killed; likewise one of the woodcocks. We
then crossed into a large island covered with high
trees and thick grass. Unluckily, on our first

entering it, we found several deer, and continued to drive them before us, frequently getting shots. Had we come to previous consultation, we should have resolved not to fire at anything but a tiger in a place so likely to be the haunt of one. About the middle of the island some elephants began to pipe in a way that assured us that they had come upon a scent. We pushed on to the end of the island, but found only a quantity of monkeys, who had been fearful of committing themselves to the rapidity of the stream. On the sand we perceived the track of a very large tiger. The footsteps were so fresh that where he had gone into the water the print was not yet washed away by the current. Agreeing to follow him, we settled not to fire at other game. We beat the thick wood of the next island closely, but fruitlessly. At the end of it we found by his traces that he still kept ahead of us. Pursuing him thus, we worked for at least three hours, but never got sight of him. We were not in the meantime blind to the beauties of the valley. It is indeed extraordinarily romantic; and even at this season the Ganges is here a grand river; there were four principal channels, with communications, which separated the interjacent islands. The eastern channel was not fordable. Everywhere the volume of water was considerable. On returning, the elephants mounted the stone steps with as much facility as they had descended them.

December 27th.—Marched to Dowlutpore. The direction was westerly, slanting from the hills. The march was marked by nothing but the sharpness of the cold. At sunrise Fahrenheit's thermometer was at 24°. Some of our sepoys were much astonished at the ice they found upon the pools or tanks.

December 28th.—Reached Secundrapoor; it has been a flourishing place, and still contains a considerable number of inhabitants. This country has not yet had time to retrieve itself after the repeated devastations it underwent in former governments.

December 29th.—Reached Saharunpoor. On the approach one is struck by the odd contrast between the neatness and show of our recent establishments and the dilapidation of all older structures. Mr. Guidall, the magistrate, and Mr.

Forrester, the registrar, had met us at Hurdwar. Mr. Colin Shakespear, the collector, received us here. In the immediate vicinity of this place the ground is bare and broken with water channels, but at a little distance there is good cultivation.

December 30th.—We went to examine the fort: it is ill situated, being nearly commanded by the jail, a strong building which, with some other enclosures protected by thick earth-banks, would be immediately seized by an enemy. The fort, however, if repaired, might be made very useful as an advanced magazine. I have therefore ordered the defences to be put in such a state as to secure it against the assault of desultory invaders. The expense of putting it into this condition can be but trifling. I then inspected the hospitals, in which there were a number of wounded from Kalunga and Jeytuk. I imagine the native troops have been unaccustomed to this kind of attention, for the poor fellows expressed their sense of it in glowing terms. I likewise examined into the treatment of the wounded Gorkha prisoners. They spoke as if they felt deeply the humanity shown to them. Their countenances are absolutely Chinese, only on

a larger scale. In the middle of the day I had a
durbar. The principal persons introduced were
Ahmad Khan and his son Khajeh Mohammad
Khan, the first uncle and the second cousin to the
late Nawab Nizabut Ali Khan; and Cooar Nulla
Sing, son of Rajah Nyne Sing, Shah Sabu Buksh,
with several of his relations, descendants of a peer
or holy man, from whom they hold a rent-free
estate in the district; Rajah Khooshal Sing, an
infant of two years old, brought by his guardian
Khoolass Roy, to receive a khelaut of investiture
on succeeding to the possessions of his father,
Rajah Ram Dial Sing, lately deceased. There
were many of inferior note. In the evening I
examined the Company's garden. The object of
retaining the spot in that form was that the
various trees and plants of the hill country might
be brought down to it; whence if they throve they
might be forwarded to the garden at Agra, and so
successively into Bengal. Little attention has been
paid towards carrying into effect this rational and
useful plan. The garden, very considerable in size,
is full of large mango-trees, all of coarse quality as
to fruit. I ordered the greater part of them to be

cut away, as likewise a large proportion of the
citron and orange-trees, which are much too numerous.   There are two distinct kinds of the former.
The lemons here have a marked difference from
those of the West Indies, and are not so good.   I
must put this garden on a better footing, for it
may be rendered extraordinarily useful.

December 31st.—Advanced to Umhacta, through
a rich, well-cultivated country.   We now saw the
snowy ridge to advantage, though the view of it
was different from that at Moradabad.   The morning was severely cold.

1815.

JANUARY 1st.—Reached Lucknontic, a place of no consequence; the march offered nothing remarkable beyond the cold. The wind blew from the snowy mountains, and we felt their influence throughout the day. We had divine service.

January 2nd.—Crossed the Jumna. Though this may perhaps be reckoned its lowest period, it is a great body of water. I forded it on my elephant. The bottom is sand. It was firm where I passed, but in other parts three or four elephants were much embarrassed by sinking in it. When an elephant is thus entangled, they give him large fascines of brushwood, and he will with his trunk place them under his leg, so as to enable himself to draw up his feet out of the quicksand. Some camels had stuck fast near the western shore. Ropes were tied round them, with the ends fastened to elephants, who readily dragged the camels out of their difficulty.   The Nawab, Ruhmut Khan, ruler of Koonjpoora, with his brother, Gholam Mohee-oo-Deen Khan, came to meet me with all his armed retinue.   We passed close along the ditch of Koonjpoora, the walls of which place are in good condition.   The scarp and counterscarp are of brick, laid pattern-wise, so as to produce a handsome effect, besides keeping the works from being washed down.   It stands the Nawab in stead to have the cantonment of Kurnaul between him and the Sikh chiefs; or the latter would soon find excuse for overpowering this Mohamedan establishment.   Rahmut Khan seemed well aware of this, and said frankly, I might well trust him, as he had not any security for his existence but in the British Government.   Our camp here (Kurnaul) is in front of the cantonment; the town lying at some little distance in the rear of our right flank.

January 4th.—I examined minutely all the environs, being strongly impressed with the necessity of always keeping together, in this country, bodies of troops capable of being opposed to an enemy on the most sudden emergency. Kurnaul has appeared to me, from its general position relatively to the

frontier, eligible as a station for such a corps.
Meerut is not only too much retired, but labours
under the disadvantage that for two months or
longer, annually, the communication between it
and Delhi or Loodheanah is cut off by the swelling
of the Jumna.   Accidental floods at other periods
render the fords impassable for some days.   The
city of Kurnaul, which has been flourishing and
considerable formerly, was reduced to the ruinous
and desolate state in which it now appears by the
same cause which had thinned the population and
destroyed the opulence of the Doab; I mean the
incessant wars urged by soldiers of fortune at the
head of predatory bands throughout the western
parts of India.   Under our Government all begins
to revive again; but there is such a conviction
in the minds of the inhabitants that a great
number of active and daring individuals scattered
through these provinces are ready to resort to any
standard which will afford the prospect of rapine,
as in a considerable degree checks confidence; and
will do so till they have had more experience of the
permanence and vigour of our Government.   I inspected the fort and the artillery depôt; essentially

they are separate buildings, but they are now connected by an outwork of earth, which is a material
security to one part of the depôt.   This latter building was a serai, for the convenience of travellers.
General Hewitt, then Commander-in-Chief, appropriated it to the use of Government, as appertain-
ing to no individual.   Lieutenant-Colonel Worsley,
then Adjutant-General, being more intimate with
the feelings of the natives, lamented the impression
likely to be made by this perversion of a charitable
establishment ; therefore he purchased a neighbouring spot of ground, and built on it, at his own expense, a serai of equal extent (though not equally
ornamented), which he made over to the city.   The
building converted into a depôt is square, with two
elegant gateways.   The arched accommodations all
round afford excellent stowage for the guns and
stores.   The roof, supported by those arches, is flat,
and forms a broad rampart walk behind a good
parapet.   An excellent ditch, secured by the fire of
towers at three of the corners, renders the defensive
state of the depôt nearly complete.   The part where
the work has not been perfected is the fourth corner, where the plan could not be continued without

destroying a large tree, under which a fakeer has taken up his residence. Leaving an object of great public concern unfinished on this account shows the attention which is paid (and wisely) to the prejudices of the natives. The intention of establishing the cantonment of a large corps at Kurnaul will render the weakness of this point of the depôt indifferent.

The fort is a small square work of somewhat greater elevation (from the ground on which it is built) than the depôt. At each angle there is a kind of bastion, whence guns would have a good range. These works are very sufficient against sudden assault. An enemy who had time and means for opening batteries against them would have great advantage in being able to approach close to them under cover. In the middle of the day I held a durbar for the Mohamedan chiefs. The Nawab Ruhmut Khan, his brother, Mohummud Khan, Ahmed Ali Khan, Mohummud Ishank Khan, Ghyrul Ali Khan, Bushurut Ali Khan, Syed Fyzoolla Shah, Meer Unwur Shah, and Meer Boorhaun Ali, were the principal.

These Affghan chiefs are fine-looking men.

They seem very solicitous to be received separately
from the Sikh chiefs, who encamped with most
numerous retinues in our neighbourhood this day,
and who are to have their audience to-morrow.

January 5th.—I traced for a considerable distance
the vestiges of the famous canal of Murdun Ali
Khan. It began where the Jumna bursts through
the hills into the plain, and it took a direction
nearly parallel to that of the river quite to Delhi.
Its object was to fertilize the long tract of country
from its source to its termination; in which extent
no tolerable water is to be procured but by sinking
wells to such an enormous depth as is beyond the
compass of ordinary funds. All the water found
in the higher strata is brackish, and is deleterious
to vegetables as well as unwholesome for man.
The stream of the Jumna in running through this
country becomes so tainted, that the necessity of
drinking it at Delhi since the canal has been destroyed, has produced great unhealthiness in the city.
This noble work of art formerly rendered the
country through which it passed an absolute garden; and the sums paid by the several villages, in
proportion to their respective population, for the

privilege of drawing water from the canal, furnished
a considerable revenue to Government. The effects
of the canal on the cultivation of the country were
so striking, that it obtained the name of the Sea of
Plenty.   During the wars which for a long period
wasted the country between the Sutlej and the
Jumna, the banks of the canal were broken in many
places, and its course stopped; so that when the
works by which the water was conducted from the
Jumna into it were destroyed by accident, no set of
men found an interest to excite their negotiating for
their restoration, or perhaps saw a chance of prevailing on the Sikhs to allow it. The country has now,
in consequence, an air of desolation.   Ruins of villages meet the eye everywhere.   There is no cultivation but close to considerable towns, where the residence of a chief and the opulence of the community
have allowed the means to be contributed for provid-
ing the neighbourhood with deep wells and good
water. The possibility of re-establishing this canal
had early struck me. I conceived that it would be an
enterprise not only dignified for our Government,
but advantageous in a high degree by procuring
us tenants for lands which no man can now have

an inducement to rent from us. The report of the engineers has been favourable beyond what I had calculated. I had assured myself that, as all the deep excavations must remain little altered, the nature of the operations for re-establishing the trunk of the canal could not be expensive, and I find I had reasoned justly. On a rough estimate the engineers compute that three lacs of rupees would suffice to put the whole of the canal into perfect condition. From their explanations I believe they have made a liberal calculation. As such an outgoing is trifling indeed in comparison to the benefits which must result from the completion of the object, I have determined on undertaking the repair immediately. The canal was close to the town and cantonments of Kurnaul, and will be inestimable to both. In the middle of the day I had my durbar. The Sikhs came in great, but truly military pomp. The Mahah Rajah Kurrum Sing, of Puttealah, was the first in rank. He is about eighteen years of age, above six feet in height, and of an open, pleasing countenance. The first impression made by his looks was not improved, and I suspect that there is not much in him. His minister,

Misser Nodha Roy, appeared to guide him altogether; so much so as to tell him to make his salaam in acknowledgment for anything courteous that I said to him. The Rajahs Bhaug Sing (Sirdar of Jheend), Bhye Laul Sing (Sirdar of Keitul), Ajeet Sing (Sirdar of Ladooah), Futteh Sing, son of the late Bhunga Sing, of Tannissar, and Gholaub Sing, nephew of the same person, were the principal chiefs.

Their manner was confident and manly, though highly respectful. Each of them presented a bow, desiring it to be observed that he added no arrow. Kurrum Sing then bade the minister step forward, and in the name of the whole explain the nature of the present. They wished it to be understood that, in delivering the bow to me, they had put the emblem of power into my hand; and that they had not offered any quiver with it, because they themselves were the arrows, to be directed at my pleasure against any foe. Finding that I spoke to them frankly and cordially, they adopted a tone of cheerful but most polite freedom, equally distant from the cautious reserve of the Mohamedan, or the timidity of the Hindoo; and they appeared extraordinarily gratified. With a good-humoured solicitation, they asked me if some of their principal officers might come into the tent and present nuzzurs, as they said the men were dying to see me. I immediately consented, and touched the nuzzurs of as many as were brought up to my chair. When this ceremony was over, I requested the Maha Rajah to accept a new-fashioned English gun, as a mark of my sense of the zeal with which he had furnished troops to Colonel Oehterlony, far beyond what he was bound to supply as his contingent. He seemed to feel the compliment much. I then apprized them of my intention to repair the canal. A general cry of " Wah !" " Wah !" (their applausive exclamation) resounded through the tent. They said it would be a blessing to millions. When I rose to give them otto, on their taking leave, they crowded about me, with looks of grateful cordiality, which gave me uncommon pleasure; for I had thence reason to think that I had hit upon the right tone with them, and that I had awakened in them a feeling of warmth towards the Company's govern-ment. We are too apt to think that these people

are swayed by the same dry, deliberate calculations
of interest which would guide us, or that they see
their advantages through the same medium with
us. It is not the case.   One need only look at
these folks to be convinced that there is a pride
about them which would make them contemn a
notion of our support, were the condition for it
presented to them in a humiliating light.   From
the specimen which I have seen of the Sikhs, I
should describe them as a bold, athletic, and
animated race. The chiefs and their attendants
were richly dressed, but in a martial way. They
all wear a scarlet turban, wreathed very close and
high, so as to be almost conical, which appears
fashioned for activity. Their several escorts of
troops were handsome and soldierlike. The Maha
Rajah produced, from his mother, some splendid
pearls for Lady Loudoun; but we made him
sensible, so that he could not take our declining
them amiss, of the reasons which obliged her in
every instance to excuse herself from the acceptance
of such presents. We parted, I believe, mutually
pleased.

January 6th.—At the entreaty of the public

secretaries, who had been most laboriously employed in preparing answers respecting voluminous despatches from Europe, transmitted by the vice-president in council, I agreed to halt here for this day. Nothing particular occurred.

January 7th.—Marched to Moonuck through a waste country, covered with scrubby trees. These were principally the dauk. It is of no use but for firewood. Being of rapid growth, what is cut away is speedily replaced; therefore, in general, the villagers cut it at pleasure. In some places, however, the zemindars, who squeeze the peasants grievously, make the people pay considerably for it.

January 8th.—Reached Suffeedan. It is fortified, but is of little strength. The Sirdar of Jheend, to whom it belongs, has a palace here; and he was now at the place, having stopped through indisposition, on his return to Jheend, after visiting me at Kurnaul. Not knowing this, Lady Loudoun went into the town to look at it, while I remained occupied with business in the camp. Bhaug Sing immediately sent his son to express the regret he felt that illness prevented his attending her himself; adding that his son was to escort her about the

town. Lady Loudoun was obliged to submit to
the civility.   When she came back and mentioned
the circumstance, I sent a complimentary message
of thanks to the young chief, and I requested his
acceptance of a double-barrelled pistol to show that
I understood the particular politeness (a homage in
their construction) of his attending her palankeen.
I rode out in the evening to examine the neighbouring country.   It did not pass unobserved; for
one of our officers overheard some of the Jheend
soldiers, who were walking in our camp and noticing
my distant movements say, " These English will
know everything."

January 9th.—Yesterday evening we heard of a
lion in the neighbourhood.

January 10th.—We encamped this day in front
of Jheend. The town covers a small hill, and it
has at a distance a showy appearance which gradually declines as a nearer approach affords a more
distinct one.   The place is fortified in a manner to
be respectable against a native force.   The fort, or
citadel, which contains the palace, is within the
town, and shouldered by the houses. As it is
built on the most elevated part of the hill, it looks

over everything.   From the manner in which the
works and buildings are huddled together in this
place, it would soon be reduced by a proper proportion of mortars.

January 13th.—Marched to Hansi. The fort
stands on an elevation considerable for this country ;
and as the hill is insulated and abrupt it is a
striking object. The Irregular Horse of Captain
Skinner, ordered to be completed to 3000, were
drawn up on my way to the camp. Their yellow
cassocks, and peculiar close turbans, have an excellent effect. The corps has a very warlike appearance. Mr. Wilder, third assistant to the Resident
of Delhi, met us here. In the afternoon I went
to examine the fort. It was the favourite strong-
hold and residence of George Thomas, well known
for having during a considerable time maintained
an independent dominion over a large tract of
territory here. All that he did within the fort was
on a scale that bespeaks an enlarged mind. The
tank in the centre of the fort, constructed to receive
and preserve the rain water, is really fine. Everything else there is in a state of sad dilapidation. As a
frontier post, Hansi is very advantageously situated ;

therefore it is expedient to keep up the fortress. The strength of it may be materially augmented by removing many of the existing works, and adding in their stead some flanking defences to the inner fort. A small garrison would then suffice for its security. At present a large body would be required to guard the fortifications against any numerous force.

January 14th.—At daybreak I went out to review the Irregular Cavalry. They bear this name because the officers have not rank on the establishment, and they are supposed to be kept in pay only for a momentary purpose. This corps, however, has been long kept in the service of the Company, and could not be dispensed with. It is only in description that it is irregular; for according to its own system, which is that of the Mahrattas, improved by Skinner, it is under strict and accurate discipline. Each man, for a certain sum monthly, provides his own horse, arms, and clothing, the two last being fixed by pattern; any man who does not keep himself properly equipped is immediately dismissed. After the corps had exhibited some manœuvres, after their fashion, the feats of the

horsemen individually were displayed. A quart
wine bottle was placed upright on the ground.
This was to serve as a mark at which the men, one
after another, were to fire, while they galloped past
it at full speed. The dexterity with which they
used their long and awkward matchlocks in this
trial was surprising. Several of them broke the
bottle; all of them shot very near it. Next they
skirmished with blank cartridges. They who pre-
tended to be beaten showed uncommon adroitness
in turning round upon their horses and firing on
their pursuers. The best part of the exhibition,
however, was the skill of some of the men in
parrying the lance with a sword. The lancer was
supposed to have gained the advantage of placing
himself on the left of the horseman whom he pursued. In that relative position, the horses going
at full gallop, the swordsman quitted his right
stirrup, and throwing his right leg over the horse
stood in the left stirrup facing to the rear, and
parrying the thrusts of the lance with the sabre.
It must not be supposed that the lancers were in-
expert. Tent-pins were driven into the ground
with a mallet, so strongly that it would have been

impossible for the most powerful arm to move them without their being previously loosened. Horsemen rode at these, and hitting them with the point of a spear forced them up from the ground.

January 15th.—We had divine service. In the middle of the day I received Jeswunt Sing, the Sikh Chief of Naba. His appearance was very respectable. I then desired to see Captain Skinner. Private information had been given to me that he had become dissatisfied with our service and proposed to resign. He is a half caste, and was formerly in the Mahratta service. On the war breaking out with them, he quitted their service in consequence of the proclamation recalling all British subjects, was employed by us, and much distinguished himself by his enterprise, his intrepidity, and his judgment. At the peace the corps commanded by him was kept in pay, and he was retained at its head. The frontier station of Hansi was assigned as its quarters. The equity and the strict observance of every promise which had marked Captain Skinner for many years, had obtained for him a prodigious influence among the natives. The loss of such a man at such a moment would be serious, especially as there is little probability that he could reconcile his mind to idleness, and it is sure that he would have most tempting offers from Holkar or Scindiah. His discontent arose from this, that the officers of Irregulars have no rank but in their own corps. Hence, if the garrison of native infantry at Hansi be reduced (as has often been the case) to a subaltern's party, Captain Skinner must find himself under the orders of possibly a very inexperienced youth. I affected not to know anything of the dispositions which he had indulged; but, beginning by a compliment to the state of his corps, I told him I wished to give a public mark of my estimation of his character. I, therefore, requested he would assume the honorary title of Lieutenant-Colonel; and I apprized him of my intention to propose to Government that such a rank in the Irregulars should entitle the officer holding it to rank as youngest field-officer of the line, and to command accordingly all captains and subalterns. I explained that as battalions were often commanded by captains, it would be easy to compose such a corps for an irregular officer in whom one had confidence, as might enable him to achieve actions meriting the highest distinctions and recompence. He appeared extraordinarily gratified, and with peculiar earnestness entreated me to rely on his unreserved devotion. To understand this warmth of feeling, one ought to know the excessive depression in which the half castes are held by the Company's servants. Till Lady Loudoun gave a private hint that colour never would be noticed, half caste ladies, though of the best education and conduct, and married to men in prominent stations, were not admitted to the Government House. Some officers have come this day from Ameer Khan's camp, bringing with them parties of their men, mounted and equipped, in order to be enrolled in Skinner's corps. Opinion of him personally has considerable weight in this; but the certainty of good treatment and regular payment is the main inducement. Skinner accepts the services of none who are not of good character within his own knowledge, or are not recommended by some officer of his corps. The persons arrived this day assert that Ameer Khan has, in his camp, 30,000 fighting men, with 125 pieces of cannon. I have in general abstained from inserting in this book any statement of public affairs, because my letter-book would afford a connected picture of such matters; but it may be well to record here what is my actual situation. With the force above mentioned, Ameer Khan has taken up a position in the territory of the Rajah of Jyepore, only twelve marches from the most important part of the Delhi district. Being grievously in want of money, he keeps this army together with great difficulty; yet he has no declared or obvious object, but incurs the distressing expense in absolute inactivity. It is clear that he is waiting in the hope of untoward events occurring to us in the Nepaulese war; an expectation founded on the extravagant opinion they entertain of the Gorkha power, and on the distorted accounts circulated respecting the reverses we have already suffered in the contest. Should he make an inroad, I can collect little more than about 4500 cavalry and infantry to put myself at the head of in order to meet him; and he must be fought as expeditiously as possible; since he might gain by delay, and I could not. It would depend on circumstances whether I could reinforce myself

with 1000 of Skinner's Horse; for it is probable
the Pindarries would make a simultaneous movement, and there is only this corps to be produced
here, the quarter in which the Pindarries would
attempt materially to penetrate.   The quality of
Ameer Khan's troops must not be misunderstood.
His cavalry is trained exactly like Skinner's, and
has been employed in petty warfare for years.   His
own artillery is good.   One of our artillery officers
who saw his horse artillery, assured me it was as
well equipped as our own.   Holkar's artillery,
which is with him, is known to be well managed.
Mohummud Khan's infantry and artillery form a
part of the corps, and are allowedly the best in
the pay of any native chieftain.   They were
both formed originally of the sepoys and Golandauzes (native artillerists) whom we improvi-
dently turned adrift in a precipitate reduction
of our forces after the Mahratta war; and they
are both said to be as accurate in discipline as
our own.   The infantry consists of six regular
battalions.   Ameer Khan has regular battalions
of his own, but not so well disciplined.   My small
force would have to assemble at Muttra, for which

it is in readiness.   I do not like to bring it
together prematurely, that its insufficiency may
not be measured by the mischievously-disposed
chieftains in our neighbourhood.   None of the
troops at Cawnpore can be moved in this direction,
as where they are they are some degree of check
on Scindiah.   He is now at Cawnpore, with not
more than 10,000 men, but he has only to reunite
those corps of his which are actually in the field,
and his army is at once fit for exertion.   At
Gwalior he is only three marches from the Doab,
five from Agra, five from Delhi.   The Pindarries,
professed freebooters, existing upon plunder, can to
a certainty bring above 20,000 horse into the field,
part of it excellent in quality.   Luckily, bitter
dissensions among themselves insure us against
their acting as one body.   Still, the cloud which
overhangs us is imposing. Such is the consequence
of the miserably inadequate establishment which
the Company allowed for the defence of this part
of its dominions.   The exigencies of the war with
the Gorkhas, whose successes have intimidated our
troops and our generals, have forced me to send
into the hills everything that was disposable,

because it would be the first step to a speedy sub-
version of our power were we to be foiled in that
struggle, and I dare not myself go thither to
remedy mismanagement, lest my quitting this
frontier should confirm the notion of our unfavourable prospects and excite an alarm in these ill-pro-
tected districts, which would of itself be enough to
invite Ameer Khan to immediate effort. With a
deeply anxious heart I am keeping up an air of indifference and confidence, and I am convinced that
I thence am supposed to possess ample resources,
though they are not immediately apparent. My
position is, however, better than it was. Some
time ago, in addition to what menaces us here,
Runjeet Sing had assembled hastily a large army
on the right bank of the Sutlej, precisely at the
place whence he last penetrated into Hindostan.
There can be no doubt but that he was tempted to
this measure by the belief that a fair opportunity
presented itself for balancing old scores with us.
We have been freed from this danger by the
most unexpected of interventions.   The King
of Cabul, in no concert with us, collected his
army and sent a message to Runjeet Sing, im-

porting that if the latter did not without delay
satisfy his Majesty respecting some territory
in debate between them, the Affghan army would
advance to Lahore. Runjeet Sing was obliged to
march immediately to his capital, whence, I understand, he means to despatch a vakeel to me with
the warmest assurances of friendship towards the
British Government. Another event, equally fortunate and equally beyond calculation, has been
of no little benefit to us in this crisis. Jean Bap-
tiste and Jeswunt Rao, generals commanding two
of Scindiah's armies, estranged by long animosities,
came to a rupture on some unimportant quarrel,
and fairly attacked each other at the head of their
respective divisions. Jeswunt Rao was beaten, and
lost many cannon. The difference is not healed,
and Scindiah's doubts whether he can depend upon
Jeswunt Rao had probably had much share in
preventing the interruption of our tranquillity.
The unfortunate Rajpoot States of Jyepore, Joud-
pore, Ondipore, mercilessly wasted by Scindiah,
Holkar, Ameer Khan, Mohummud Shah Khan,
and the Pindarries, have assailed me with repeated
petitions to take them under protection as feuda-

tories to the British Government. The inexplicable treaty by which Sir G. Barlow, without receiving any consideration for the pledge, bound this Government in an engagement with Scindiah and Holkar not to interfere in any way with the Rajpoot States, would render it a direct breach of public faith were we to take a step equally counselled by a generous humanity and by an unquestionable interest.

January 16th.—We set out on our march. We found our tents pitched at Chota (little) Bhowannee.

January 17th.—Although we were told that all the country parallel to the march we had to make this day, was so devoid of cover as to afford no prospect of meeting a lion, the knowledge that we were after this day to enter a country so highly cultivated as to preclude the possibility of finding them, made us resolve not to throw away even the poor chance which we still had. At about seven miles wide of our road, two curious hills, apparently composed of loose blocks of stone, arose from the plain. We thought there might be cover about their bases, but there was not any on the side which we approached. These hills, now perceived by us to be the beginning of a chain which connects with the Alwar elevations, have clearly been produced by some kind of eruption which has forced up the strata of stone, and accumulated them in fragments in these detached heaps. Foiled in our hope, the forwardness of the day would have recommended that we should strike for the main road which led towards our camp. In that line, however, we could see there was not a bush. About six miles a-head of us, there appeared trees which we supposed to be a thicket. We resolved to push for it. In our way we fell in with some large herds of cattle. The men attending them, of the tribe of Jhaats, informed us that the trees to which we were steering only surrounded a village, but that they could show us, at about two miles from where we then were, a place where there was great probability of our finding a lion. They told us that they had of late often seen two, which had carried off many of their cows.

It is extraordinary how little apprehension these people have of the lion. They say it never wantonly attacks a man; so that if it gets enough of other food, and they do not provoke it, they are

not terrified at seeing it prowling about. Then
they always say to you, if it be my destiny to be
eaten by a lion, no care of mine will prevent it;
he will come and take me out of my bed. Leaving
the cattle under the charge of some boys, three or
four men went to show the place where they thought
it likely our game should be found.

There never was a more promising spot. It was
a dell, which ran from the back of the first hill,
and it was full of long grass and thorns. We beat
it with the utmost care, refraining from firing at
other animals, which continually started up before
us, but found no lion. We then returned to the
herds. I this day remarked what I had indeed
observed on many former occasions, what a fine
race of men the Sikhs and Jhaats are. They are
not bulky, but they are tall and energetic. Their
step is firm and elastic; their countenances frank,
confident, and manly; and their address has much
natural politeness. I had noticed the same appearance in the Rohillas and Patans, but with less of
cheerful air than what I observe in the Sikhs.
More active, brave, and sturdy fellows can nowhere be found than these tribes present. The

man who more particularly attached himself to me as my guide on this occasion had rich gold ear-rings beautifully wrought, though he had on no other article of dress than a pink turban and a wrapper round his loins. When we approached the herd, we observed at about two hundred yards' distance from it a patch of between eight and ten acres in extent, covered with low straggling thorns, with here and there a large bush clothed with ever-green bindweed, but the cover was so thin, and there were so many cattle tracks through it, that in England one should not have looked for a fox in such a place. More from the principle of leaving nothing untried than from the supposition that there was any chance of finding a lion there, we directed our course through the thorns. When we had got nearly to the further end, two lionesses started up before us. Some ineffectual shots were fired, and both the animals took to the plain. One, at which both my rifles missed fire, gained a little ravine at some distance, which we took for granted must yield her a secure escape. The other afforded us a curious spectacle.

There was so little expectation of our finding a lion

there, that one of Skinner's Irregular horsemen (a party of whom attended us at a distance) was riding up to the thorns to deliver a letter which had been sent after me. The lioness made a dash at him, though her distance from him was considerable. He made off with all the speed to which his spurs could rouse the horse. The lioness coursed him fairly in the open plain, and gained so much upon him as to give us extreme uneasiness. At length, by the time he had reached a little rising ground, his horse got into his rate, and the lioness found she could not overtake him. She then turned round the point of the hill over which he had gone straight. Just at that moment, all the herdsmen who had followed us called to us, and said that the first lioness had come back into the thorns. We had no difficulty in finding her. The gentleman who first stumbled on her wounded her. Though she was much crippled by the shots, when I met her, on turning round a bush, she made a gallant run at my elephant. I, luckily, hit her in the head, and she fell immediately. At that moment the screams of the herdsmen made us turn round, and we beheld the other lioness galloping through the midst of them to regain the cover. Though she passed close to three or four, she did not attempt to strike at any of them, but hastened to take refuge in the longest and best covered bush that the place afforded. I caused my elephant, which was a powerful one, to be pushed at her citadel. The elephant intrepidly forced its head into the bush, when some other elephants could not be brought to approach it. The lioness was growling in a tone which gave them to understand that she might revenge an insult. The thorns were so excessively interlaced that my elephant could not force its way to the centre of the bush. My head was above the leafy covering, and I never could discover the animal, but I was quite sensible of the efforts made by my elephant to reach the lioness with its foot, and trample on it, an attempt which was prevented from succeeding by the toughness and intertexture of the stems. I fired three shots at random, and hearing no more noise, imagined I had despatched the animal. I therefore directed my mohout to go to the other side of the bush where I thought it might be more practicable to obtain a view. Just as I got round, the lioness darted out, and springing at the elephant on which Mr. Shakespear was riding, fixed her talons in each of its ears while she vigorously assailed its forehead with her teeth.   The violent exertions of the elephant to get rid of this troublesome appendage put into confusion all the elephants that were near, and prevented help being given.   But it had a still worse effect; for in one of its ungovernable efforts, the elephant threw Mr. Shakespear out of the howdah.   Luckily, he fell on a bush, so that he was not hurt, yet he rolled to the ground, and there lay exposed.   Two of Skinner's horsemen seeing his situation most gallantly drew their sabres and galloped forward to protect him.   At the same instant the lioness was thrown off, but happily on the side opposite to that where Mr. Shakespear lay. On recovering herself, her attention was attracted by the haunches of an elephant which had wheeled round through fear close to her.   She seized it, and tore the inside of both its thighs dreadfully.   There was now, however, an opportunity of firing at her, and she received three or four wounds.   Checked by these, she retired into the bush; she could not be seen there; but so many shots were fired into

it on chance, that some could not have avoided
hitting her. Wearied with this annoyance, she
slunk out into some thinner cover. My elephant
soon reached the place; and I saw her lying exhausted. She roused herself and attempted to
come towards me; but I believe the effort would
have been vain had I not given her another shot,
which was instantly decisive. It was with great
difficulty that we brought to our camp, at Great
Bhowannee, the elephant whose thighs had been so
lacerated. Its loss of blood was excessive. In our
way home we saw many bustards; they appear to
differ from the English bustard only in the amplitude of a loose black topping and some long flossy
white feathers round the neck. They were extraordinarily shy. I observed this day one of those
effects of whirlwind described by Bence. Three or
four minor gusts had raised the dust at different
times, and carried it up in a column the height
of many feet. At last, one at some distance from
us raised a perfect column that could not have been
less than three score feet high; probably much
more. The sun shining on the dust gave it a
gilded appearance. It was quite thin, as I could

perceive by the way in which the dust fell when the gust no longer supported it. I imagine the pillars of moving sand supposed to be so fatal occasionally to caravans are equally innoxious.

January 18th.—Our lionesses were measured last night; one was nine feet four inches from the nose to the tip of the tail; the other two inches less. In such a measurement the tail of the lion furnishes less than that of the tiger to the general amount. Anxious interest, as had been the case on a former occasion, was made with our servants for a bit of the flesh, though it should be of the size of a hazel-nut. Every native in the camp, male or female, who was fortunate enough to get a morsel, dressed it and eat it. They have a thorough conviction that the eating a piece of lion's flesh strengthens the constitution incalculably, and is a preservative against many particular distempers. This superstition does not apply to tiger's flesh, though the whiskers and claws of that animal are considered as very potent for bewitching people. Our native attendants (I have been assured) do not at all like that those articles should get into our hands, though they cannot exactly tell in what

manner the misapplication of the power by us is
dreaded by them. Our march this day was to
Dadree. The Nawab Fyze Mohummud Khan, ordinarily called the Nawab of Narnoul, had come
forward to that town (which belongs to him) to
pay his attentions. It was settled that he should
breakfast with me; and that in the afternoon,
when I rode to look at the town, I should pay him
a short visit. The Nawab, with his uncle Fyze
Tullub Khan, administrator during the Nawab's
minority, and two of the Nawab's brothers, met us
about the middle of the march. The riding-dresses
of them all were very handsome, and they appeared good horsemen. On approaching the town,
we discovered a considerable line of troops drawn
up. There were two corps of cavalry, a battalion
of sepoys equipped like ours, a strong regiment
of nujeebs, or regular matchlock men, with four
pieces of cannon. They all looked very well.
Some bodies of the Nawab's troops are at this
instant doing duty for us at frontier stations,
whence we have been obliged to withdraw our
infantry for service against the Gorkhas.

As I passed along the line, some of the sepoys

quitted the ranks, and attempted to run forward
to my elephant, but were stopped by their officers.
On my arrival in camp, the Nawab and his attendants were not forthcoming; I soon learnt that we
were not likely to have their company, for the
troops had mutinied and seized them. It was to
complain of being grievously in arrear of pay that
the men had attempted to get to me. In order to
prevent any explanation of this to me, or any
further attempt to state their wrongs, the Nawab
had stayed behind. Approaching the infantry to
harangue them, he with his suite found themselves
suddenly enveloped and prisoners. It was my
policy to feign ignorance of the event, that I
might not be under the necessity of an awkward
intervention. I detached Lieutenant-Colonel Skinner privately, to endeavour at conciliating the
men. This he effected readily. His simple assurance that he would see justice done to them
quieted the business immediately, and emancipated
the personages who had been held in restraint.
The poor Nawab was not to be persuaded that I
must not be furious against him for this scene,
and his uncle was not less so. I quieted them by

a message, assuring them that I was not absolutely outrageous, and that (although it would not be fitting for me to go into Dadree while there was a possibility of the ferments recommencing) I would take an early opportunity of showing him attention. In the afternoon, I received Ruhmut Ali Khan, son of the late chief of Malwar Khotelah. These interviews have effect beyond the mere fulfilment of empty form. The feudatory Chiefs and Jagheerdars, from even that slight intercourse, feel themselves more personally connected with the Government; and the homage which they pay is a plighted fidelity before the public.

January 19th.—We marched to Hussein Gunje. This is a little town which had been fortified with mud walls and four round bastions, by George Thomas. It is now within the territory of Fyze Mohummud Khan. Soon after my arrival an express followed from him to inform me that an arrangement had been made with which the troops had been entirely satisfied. In the middle of the day, I was apprized that he had come to the town, beyond which our camp stood at about a mile's distance, for the purpose of being near enough to render any service that we might require. To repay this attention, I mounted my horse in the afternoon, and rode to the town. Just as I had entered the gate, I met him hurrying afoot with the rest of his family to it. He and his uncle appeared exceedingly confused and depressed. I got off my horse immediately, and embracing them both before all the people, restored their spirits. The Nawab is about nineteen, rather stout, and well looking, and of good manners. His brothers are much younger. The uncle is a manly, gallant, and sagacious fellow. I had been grieved that anything had affected the pride he naturally indulged in displaying a well appointed little force which was always at the requisition of our Government, therefore I strove to dispel any notion of discredit which might have been taken up by his followers. The inside of the town was wretched. I walked with the Nawab to the poor mansion in which he had taken up his quarters, and sat down with him. A rich sword, with a tray of jewels, and various other articles, were brought for me, with another tray of diamonds

and rubies for Lady Loudoun. I reminded him
that I had accepted his peshcush (a present understood 'to convey a profession of fealty,) when he
had put himself to the trouble of so long a march
as the coming to see me at Moradabad; that he
must perceive I had not been insensible to his zeal
on that occasion; that a second peshcush was unnecessary where reciprocal kindness existed, and
my acceptance of it would be to subject him to an
useless expense, but that in token of friendship I
would take one article. I fixed on a pair of Cashmere stockings. They appeared to be of a very
fine sort of felt, composed of pretty long light
brown hair, exceedingly soft and pliant. In walking back towards the entrance of the town, we
met my children, and I introduced them to him.
On reaching the gate, I again embraced him, his
uncle, and his brothers, and bade him a good
evening.

January 20th.—Four of our servants had set out
in the middle of the night to reach our new camp
at Dholera at an early hour, in order to have our
breakfast ready when we should arrive. They
were on a pad elephant, and for the purpose of

avoiding the dust, had chosen not to go with a party of servants which regularly proceeded under protection of an escort about the same hour. They came back before day, in desperate trepidation. They reported that when they got half way, the elephant was stopped by two large animals, who approached it growling and roaring furiously; that these beasts walked round them several times; that the elephant fell into a violent trembling, which was fully answered by their own muscles, and that the elephant had at last fairly run away with them back to Hussein Gunje. The mohout confirmed the story, declaring that his fears had absolutely petrified him, and that he did not recover the use of either his judgment or his hands till he had got at least two miles from the spot where they had been beset. From the account, I should imagine that the elephant had at first showed much steadiness, and remained firm, till he found that his riders were not of the same way of thinking with him. The animals must have been tigers; for we are now in the midst of a cultivated tract, and lions (as I learn) never come into a country of that description. The vast plains of

Hurreanah, where nothing interrupts their loco-
motive disposition, are exactly suited to them.
That immense district is the finest for a sportsman
I have ever seen, and I should have had singular
gratification in being able to indulge myself in a
few days more of shooting there. The pressure of
many vital concerns allowed me no such scope. It
is observable, from the experience of that country,
that where there are lions a tiger is scarcely ever
seen; so that one has to suspect the former has the
mastery. The tiger, however, exceeds in bulk and
apparent strength the Asiatic lion. It has not,
indeed, the same elastic gait; and I should think
there may be a vivacity in the courage of the lion
which might alone render the neighbourhood uncomfortable to the tiger, though he were essentially
stronger. The natives evidently believe in the
superiority of the lion; for in those parts where we
have been sporting they have no name for the
animal but bura sheer, the greater tiger. Encouraged by the report of our frightened servants, we
tried the country parallel with the line of march,
at the distance of about a mile from the road; but
we found no place where it was likely a tiger should

lie. The whole tract, in the direction which we took, with a great width to each side, is highly cultivated. I was conscious of a curious sensation. Some time ago, the expectation of meeting a tiger would have been one of the most eager possible. Now the game appeared secondary to a lion, and the anxiety had proportionally diminished. We reached Dholera, a poor place, affording nothing worthy of observation.

January 21st.—Proceeded to Bahadurghur. As our tents were pitched beyond it, I rode through the town to reach it. It has formerly been a place of no mean rate, but it has fallen much into decay. The walls are still kept up in tolerable order, though it has never been strong. The ground on which our camp was fixed appeared all undermined by some small animal. If, in riding, one did not keep to a beaten path, one's horse sunk continually into the burrows.

January 22nd.—Soon after midnight a most violent rain came on and lasted till seven this morning. The deluge, by filling the burrows, forced the poor tenants of them to come out in numbers and seek shelter in our tents. The animal is a large species of dormouse, about the size of a half-grown rat, of a cream-colour, with very prominent black eyes, and a tuft of hair at the end of the tail. The little creatures showed no fear of us, and only quietly moved aside as we approached them. I believe their confidence commanded safety for them, so that few if any of them were hurt in the camp. Mr. Metcalfe arrived from Delhi. The King had been carrying on a wearisome negotiation with him to obtain that I should visit him. Mr. Metcalfe always returned the same answer,—namely, that I had expressed myself as very desirous of paying my personal attentions to his Majesty; but had told him (Mr. Metcalfe) that I was restrained from doing so by the knowledge that his Majesty expected my acquiescence in a ceremonial which was to imply his Majesty's being the liege lord of the British possessions. This dependent tenure, Mr. Metcalfe assured him, could never be acknowledged by me. The King tried a variety of modifications as to the particular form in which his suzerainty over the Company's territories was to be asserted; but at length, after Mr. Metcalfe's assuring him that the more or the less of the distinctions to be shown to me could have no effect where my resistance was to the admission of any foreign supremacy over our dominions, his Majesty at length gave up the hope of a meeting. This procedure on my part was dictated not more by the tenure of the recent Act of Parliament which declares the sovereignty of the Company's possession to be in the British Crown, than by a clear conviction of our impolicy in keeping up the notion of a paramountship in the King of Delhi. It is dangerous to uphold for the Mussulmans a rallying-point, sanctioned by our own acknowledgment that a just title to supremacy exists in the King of Delhi. Were the two elder brothers of Prince Jehangeer to die before the King, their issue becomes by the Mohamedan law cut out from the succession. Jehangeer would then, according to the principle of primogeniture, which we have maintained, ascend the throne whensoever his father should die. We should then find that we had invested a young vigorous man, who cherishes the deepest animosity towards us, with unquestioned right to call on the native sovereigns for support against our oppressive encroachments on his rule. We should have difficulty in making out a good case consistently with our own theory; and the practical part of the business might be no less embarrassing. The house of Timour had been put so much out of sight, that all habit of adverting to it was failing fast in India; and nothing has kept up the floating notion of a duty owed to the imperial family but our gratuitous and persevering exhibition of their pretensions—an exhibition attended with much servile obeisance in the etiquettes imposed upon us by the ceremonial of the court. I have thence held it right to discountenance any pretension of the sort, either as it applies to us or to any of the native princes. It is now decided that I do not go to Delhi. A deputation will immediately proceed thither to offer my compliments to his Majesty.

January 23rd.—I rode out at daybreak. In the direction which I took there is little attempt at cultivation. The country is a sandy expanse, all undermined by the dormice. How such multitudes of those animals support themselves, where so few vegetables of any sort appear, is not easy to be solved. In the middle of the day I held a durbar.

Fyze Mohummud Khan (to whom Bahadurghur belongs), with his uncle, Fyze Tullub Khan, came to take leave, and appeared very grateful. The Nawab, Vizeer Khan, ruler of Malore; Kotelah, and his cousin Fuzl Ali Khan, were present; the latter is brother of Ruhmut Ali Khan, who was introduced at Dadree. The Nawab Mohummud Mozuffur Khan, a child, was brought in the arms of his maternal grandfather, Ilahee Buksh Khan, to receive the khelaut of investiture as chief of Furrucknuggur. The poor little fellow cried bitterly when a rich heavy turban was put on his head. Ray Bhowanee Shunker, Istumrardar of Nujufghur; Mohummud Fyze Deen Khan, Jagheerdar of Tickree; Thakoor Doss, son of Thakoor Dya Ram of Hattrass; Ajadheea Purshaud, Khazanchy of the Delhi Residency; and Hakeem Boo Ali Khan, an old highly-respected physician of Delhi, who had been very anxious to see me, were the other principal persons.

January 24th.—Riding out along the road towards Delhi, I found the country almost as waste as on the other side of Bahadurghur. Want of water occasions the deficiency of population, and

consequent activity. Unless the wells here are
sunk to a depth requiring an expenditure beyond
the means of individuals (those wells being at the
same time lined with brick to prevent the entrance
of water from the upper strata), the springs are
found so impregnated with salt, as to be quite
unfit for drinking; and the application of such
water to the soil is here found injurious to vegeta-
tion. Branches from the projected canal would
fertilize all this tract. The canal which bore the
name of Firozeshah, ran from the great canal into
Hurreanah, some miles beyond Hansi. I looked
at its vestiges, and have ever since been anxious to
dispossess the lions, by re-establishing the villages,
to which such a supply of water had formerly
given birth. The natural fertility of that soil is
great. In the rainy season, a rich succulent grass
covers the plains. It makes excellent hay. I saw
at Lieutenant-Colonel Skinner's farm two stacks,
each calculated for the maintenance of forty mares
(he has a breeding stud) through the winter.
The price which he paid for collecting the grass,
making the hay, bringing it to his farm-yard, and
stacking it, was sixty-four rupees (£8) for each stack.

January 25th.—We had intended to move to-day to Nureela, whence Lady Loudoun was to proceed to Delhi, and I was to repair to Meerut. Lady Loudoun was so unwell in the night that I countermanded the march. The deputation to the King of Delhi was, however, despatched. It consisted of Mr. Ricketts, Mr. Adam, and Mr. Swinton, secretaries of Government; Mr. Thomson, private secretary; Major Doyle, military secretary; Honourable Major Stanhope, first aide-de-camp; and my nephew, the Honourable William Moore. These gentlemen were instructed to present nuzzurs on their own individual account, as had been done to me by the members of the King's deputation at Moradabad, but they were not to offer any nuzzur from me. It used to be the etiquette for the Resident on particular occasions to present to the King a nuzzur from the Governor-General, as a homage from the latter to his liege lord. This custom I have abrogated: considering such a public testimony of dependence and subservience as irreconcileable to any rational policy.

January 26th.—Marched to Nareela, a country improving in cultivation as we approached it. We here met the Begum Somroo, who had advanced thus far from her jagheer on the other side of the Jumna, to pay her compliments. This extraordinary woman was purchased when a girl by Somers, the German, infamous for having lent himself as the instrument for murdering the British prisoners at Patna, after the native sirdars had revolted at the order. That man was one of the description of Europeans frequent at the time, who used to hire themselves to the Indian princes, with a little band of native troops better armed and disciplined than was the case with the rest of the soldiery composing the armies.

These men were like the Italian condottieri of old. In proportion to the quality and reputation of their corps, they demanded a large sum for attaching themselves to the cause of any great chieftain; and the exigencies of the latter produced ready acquiescence in the unconscionable terms. Paying to their men with a punctuality unprecedented in Indian armies the moderate wages at which they had engaged those followers, they secured to their service a decided preference, while they had at disposal ample balances, which they applied in the purchase of more muskets and accoutrements for the augmentation of their corps. Somers, however atrocious, appears to have been acute and sagacious. He gradually improved his fortunes, till his assistance became a matter of importance to the Emperor. The naturally quick understanding of his wife had been strengthened and expanded by the education which he had given her the means of attaining, and she became a most active and judicious assistant to him in all his most intricate concerns. She took the field with him, and in action was borne in her palankeen from rank to rank, encouraging the men, who were enchanted with her heroism. The essential service which she rendered to Shah Allum made him confer on her a life-interest, in survivance to her husband, in the considerable district assigned to Somers for the maintenance of his troops; Shah Allum further dignified her with the title of Begum or Princess. Since the death of her husband, she has managed the jagheer, the revenues of which exceed £150,000 a year, with great ability; maintaining in good order a considerable number of troops, preserving a tolerable police in the district, and keeping up her own authority firmly. The jagheer being within the territory ceded to the Company, the Begum is now our feudatory. Troops of hers are employed in taking care of many of the places whence we have withdrawn those regiments of ours employed on the Nepaulese frontiers. The Begum dined with us. As she is a Christian, none of our dishes came amiss to her; and good Madeira wine is peculiarly acceptable to her palate. She has the remains of a fine face, with a fairer complexion than is frequent among the natives, and peculiarly intelligent eyes. Her head must always, I think, have been out of proportion to her body; for it is large, and she is short beyond what one can ascribe to sinking from age. She insists on escorting me across her district to Meerut. I expected she would rather have accompanied Lady Loudoun to Delhi, but she roundly told us she did not like to go near the royal family, as she, in that case, must pay her visit in the zenana, and would be mercilessly squeezed for presents.

January 27th.—Crossed the Jumna at Baughput, and encamped on the northern bank. On that

side there is a handsome Hindoo ghaut, with
the usual accompanying temples.   There is probably a good endowment, for there were many
fakeers among the buildings.   The ford at this
season is very good, the streams being not either
broad or deep, and the bottom hard.   The cultivation on this side is good.   The Begum encamped
about a quarter of a mile from our tents.   In the
afternoon I rode to pay her a visit.   Her tent was
small and simple; and the troops of her escort,
well drawn out for show, made a good appearance.

January 28th.—Encamped at Poorah, on the
further bank of the Kalee Nuddee.   This river runs
between the Jumna and the Ganges, parallel to
each till it takes the turn which leads it into the
latter, some distance below Furruckabad.   The
straightness of its course, and the depth of the
water, qualities which I understand distinguish it
throughout its extent, ought to render it extraordinarily useful for transporting the produce of the
Doab to distant markets; yet I do not learn that
much advantage of the kind is drawn from it.
Where we passed the ford was sound, but the water
high.

January 29th.—Arrived at Meerut. The approach to it, over a waste plain, is not calculated to impress one with a favourable prepossession. The troops were out to receive me, and looked remarkably well. The division consists of the King's Royal Irish Dragoons, the 3rd and 7th Regiments of Native Cavalry, two battalions of Grenadiers, and two troops of Horse Artillery. Breakfasted with Major-General Sir William Keir, at present in command here. Attended divine service. There is no church, and the service is performed in one of the barrack bungalows, a building quite unfit for the purpose. The tenour of the sermon was to impress upon us the strict and defined repartition of functions between the different persons of the Trinity; a line which, we were assured, would be inviolably preserved from the indelicacy which each must feel would attend the trespassing on the prerogatives of another.

January 30th.—I had all the troops of the station out this morning for the performance of some manœuvres, which they executed remarkably well. In the middle of the day I had a levee for the Europeans, civil and military. In the afternoon

I reviewed the two battalions of Grenadiers, and found them in excellent order.

January 31st.—This morning I reviewed the King's 8th Light Dragoons. It is a noble regiment, always distinguished for high spirit, and at present in an admirable state of discipline. Before I returned to my tent I went and examined the regimental schools. I had yesterday visited the hospitals, which I forgot to insert. I had great reason to be pleased with them, as was the case also this day with regard to the children, among whom I found many striking instances of proficiency. At noon I held a durbar. There were presented some of the respectable natives of the neighbourhood; but the principal person was the vakeel from Runjeet Sing. That prince, aware of the awkward colour which his assembling an army on the Sutlej must bear, endeavours to remove the impression of his projected hostility by exaggerated attentions. The vakeel is charged to express Runjeet Sing's regret that I had not approached near enough to the Sutlej to allow of his coming in person to see me. The most earnest assurances of his friendship are given, and he has sent presents

more than ordinarily splendid, which of course are
accepted by the Company.   I, with a sincerity
equal to his own, professed the most unbounded
confidence in the Maha Rajah's amicable dispositions, was as courteous as possible to the vakeel,
and clothed him in a very rich khelaut.   In the
afternoon I reviewed the Horse Artillery; a very
well trained and equipped corps.   After I had
despatched them I reviewed the two regiments of
Native Cavalry; so that this has not been an idle
day.   Lieutenant-Colonel Knox was the senior
officer, and showed perfect knowledge in his management of the cavalry.   I was much pleased with them.

February 1st.—Marched to Begumabad through
a country principally desert.   Many wild date-
trees scattered over portions of it, give it a resemblance to what one has heard of the Arabian
wastes.   The Begum Sumroo had insisted, notwithstanding every decent endeavour on my part
to escape from the embarrassing attention, on accompanying me.   The plea was that she had not
taken formal leave of Lady Loudoun.   Of course
I insisted that she should be my daily guest on this
march, as she had been in our progress to Meerut.

She is shrewd, and used to amuse us with sly remarks on public personages whom she had known.

February 2nd.—Marched to Dansah. We had scarcely reached our camp when heavy rain came on.

February 3rd.—The rain continued all night. As it appeared to have cleared away in the morning, I ordered tents to be struck. We had not proceeded above three miles when the rain began again. It continued till we arrived at Soorijpoor, fourteen miles from our last encampment.

February 4th.—The morning was clear, and we marched to Dankoor, where I proposed fording the Jumna. The river, however, had swelled suddenly, and the ford was impassable. We therefore pitched our tents, and I went out with three or four gentlemen to beat some jungle along the bank of the river said to be likely for game. The jungle was so filled with water that all the animals had been driven out. We therefore turned up into the country, which we found generally well cultivated. One of our party shot a partridge, which fell at some distance from shore into a large and deep jheel, or lake. The mohout of one of the elephants, which we had brought out to assist us in beating, immediately put his beast into the water, and the elephant swam to the partridge very quietly; no sooner, however, was the bird got, than the elephant turned on its side, and in that position swam back to land. None of the party had ever before seen an elephant swim in that way. We came on some pretty extensive salt works of curiously simple structure. The vats were formed by little banks of clay enclosing a spot on the harder part of the soil; the brine was raised from a well by a bucket and hand-wheel, and the sun exhaled the water from the vat, leaving the salt dry. In passing the jheel on our return I saw an enormous alligator on the bank. I got my elephant near enough to have a fair shot. I hit it with one of the large balls. It rolled off the bank into the water; but although the place was very deep, it continued for several seconds floundering violently on the surface. It then sank and disappeared.

February 5th.—The river having fallen during the night, we forded it this morning, and proceeded to Koor-Ali. The country on the right bank of the river presented one of the richest scenes I have ever beheld. As far as the eye could

reach in every direction the plain was covered with
a luxuriant crop of wheat.   The villages scattered
here and there, all enveloped with trees, break the
uniformity of the surface without interrupting
the display of plenty which we witnessed.   Having
breakfasted at Koor-Ali, I mounted my horse,
and rode across the country for Lady Loudoun's
camp at Sikrie.   It was about fourteen miles from
Koor-Ali, and she was to reach it this day on her
way from Delhi.   At a little village on the road,
I stumbled on the Rajah of Bulumghur, who was
coming in great pomp to visit me at Koor-Ali.
Our interview was much less formal than he had
expected.   He had descended from his elephant,
and come forward with his nuzzur, before I knew
whom we had met.   Presents were called for by
him; but I begged that he would be contented
with my taking the matchlock and tulwar (always
very ordinary ones) which are tendered on such
occasions in token of feudal adherence.   The for-
bearing to accept those articles would be construed
into slighting the attachment professed. He wanted
to hang a most beautiful string of pearls on the
tulwar, but I would not allow it.   Then he said

he must follow me to Sikrie to pay his homage more formally. I showed him a prodigiously heavy cloud approaching, and I advised him to get back to Bulumghur with all speed before we should be deluged with its contents, adding that I claimed his obedience to the instruction. He seemed much gratified in being treated with this cheerful frankness, and we parted with much cordiality. I fear the finery of the poor Rajah and his suite must have suffered sadly; for, although I rode hard, before I reached Sikrie the rain came down in torrents. This Rajah is a young man with an uncommonly mild and amiable countenance.

February 6th.—The ground on which we were encamped being low, the rain made it very swampy, and the Quartermaster-General was anxious that we should get away from it. He therefore sent forward part of the baggage last night, though the appearances of change in the weather were by no means decided. About two o'clock in the morning the rain came on again with excessive violence. Unable to strike our tents, we have been obliged to remain here, the camp standing in a sheet of water.   I have got Lady Loudoun and the children into a small tent, which occupies a little sort of knoll, occasioned probably by the ruins of two or three mud-houses.   It has continued raining all day.

February 7th.—The sky having cleared, we set out on our march.   A prodigious quantity of water lay upon our road.   The soil was unluckily of a nature to become very slippery when wet; and it was painful to see that many of our camels had perished from falling with their loads.   They were probably hurt by the fall, but they were also sickened by the rain, and seem not to struggle to keep their heads out of the splashes of water, so that they are readily smothered.   The excessive unsteadiness of a camel's footing in wet ground is the great defect of that useful animal.   The Nawab, Moorteza Khan, who is Jagheerdar of Pulwul, met us about halfway, and presented his nuzzur.   He was in armour, as were his principal attendants. The appearance was picturesque and showy.   His troops, drawn up by the side of the road, looked very well.   He wished to attend me to camp on horseback at the head of his cavalry; but, as I was on my elephant, I desired he would get on his, which I saw in waiting. After he had made many excuses respecting its being too great a liberty, he yielded; and I was pleased to see that he took two little boys, his sons, into the howdah with him. When we reached camp, he entreated earnestly that he might make a refayut; that is, that he might be allowed to feed the troops and camp-followers for the day. I would not suffer him to incur so unnecessary an expense. He would have had above 10,000 mouths to fill; for, although we have but one battalion of infantry, and one hundred and sixty of the bodyguard, a bazaar has attached itself to us large enough to supply the wants of any army. All trades, even working jewellers, are to be found in the camp.

February 8th.—The wet condition of the tents and baggage, with the fatigue of the cattle, required our halting this day.

February 9th.—Our cattle had suffered so much from the rain that the Quartermaster-General requested another day's halt for them. Mr. Metcalfe returned to Delhi, taking Mr. Stirling with him.

February 10th.—The troops of Moorteza Khan accompanied us to the limits of his jagheer, which was near our camp at Buncharee, a village in the vicinity of Hoorool. There we were met by Ahmud Buksh Khan at the head of his little force. I have mentioned him at Moradabad; and I was really glad to see him again, as the frank manliness of his manners had struck me much. He seemed no less pleased at the meeting. I gave audience to-day to Irteza Khan and his nephew, Yakoob Ali Khan, persons of family residing at Delhi.

February 11th.—We set out for Chattah. Ahmud Buksh Khan with his troops escorted us. As we approached the camp, his oont-surwars (camel-riders) went a-head of us. They are armed with a large blunderbuss fixed on a swivel on the pommel of the saddle. With this artillery they gave us a salute as we passed. One of the blunderbusses burst, and hurt the chin of the poor fellow who fired it. I ordered the surgeon of the bodyguard to attend him, and sent the man some money. The manner in which this little attention, though there is not one of our countrymen who would have omitted it, was felt by Ahmud Buksh's soldiers, gives reason to suspect that under such accidents the natives receive but poor commiseration from their own people. It shows also that there is such a propensity in them to overrate every act of kindness from persons in high station, as may make one wonder that the general run of princes stand so moderately in favour with the multitude. I had here a durbar to receive Rajah Puddun Sing, a man of great respectability, and Zoolfecar Ali, vakeels from Rao, Rajah of Macherry. They brought presents of much richness and nice selection, and were extraordinarily gratified when I made observations on the elegance of pattern or delicate workmanship of any of the articles. This trifling urbanity, which they have been rarely accustomed to meet, is not thrown away. Our people are too dry with the natives. The latter give us high credit for justice, but I fear they regard us in general as very repulsive. Ahmud Buksh Khan, in armour as being on my guard, Moorteza Khan with his family, Fyze Oolla Beg Khan and his son Nukshbund Khan, attended the durbar, and we had cheerful conversation.

February 12th.—Fyze Oolla Beg Khan escorted

us to Chomah with his troops.   Each of these jagheerdars maintains out of pride a much greater number of soldiers than that to which he is bound by the tenure of his jagheer.   It is a disposition useful to us; for these feudatories are ready and active in employing their men to repress tumults, or disperse predatory gangs in our territories on the call of the magistrate.   Mr. Turner, Mr. Wright, and Mr. McSween have here met us from Agra.   Divine service as usual.

February 13th.—We marched to Bindrabund. After breakfast, we went from our camp, about a quarter of a mile from the walls, to see the temples of this sacred city.   It is esteemed the birthplace of Krishna, though other spots have contested that honour.   The oldest of the temples is quite gone to ruin.   The vestiges do not even enable one to make out what it has been; but a special sanctity is attached to the ground within the walls which surround the space where it stood.   Numerous priests attend it.   Their time is principally occupied in feeding a prodigious number of monkeys which inhabit the ruins.   Another temple, which has been of much superior magnificence, exhibits inter-

z 2

esting remains. It is built of a red stone resembling a coarse marble. Much labour in carving, though little elegance of architecture, has decorated the out-side. The interior of the building reminds one strik-ingly of our old cathedrals. The figure of Krishna, richly dressed, occupies the chancel. The distribu-tion and many of the ornaments of the body of the church have much connexion with what we see in our antique Gothic edifices. This is upon the best scale of any building I have seen appropriated to Hindoo purposes. It is probably the work of Affghans who, prior to the time of Mohamed, embraced the religion of the country which they conquered. From this temple we went to visit the mesjid or mosque built by Aurungzebe on the spot where Krishna was born. A Hindoo temple of peculiar fame and sanctity identified the position of that interesting event. It is an elevated knoll, commanding the town and adjacent country. The intolerant Moslem levelled the temple and built on its site a heavy mosque of red stone, which, though apparently much neglected, through the indiffer-ence of Krishna and his devotees, remains unharmed. The more modern piety of the Hindoos has been active in raising here buildings called thoongs, which, though receptacles for one or other of the deities of their mythology, are rather monuments to a parent or ancestor. Himmut Bahadur's and the Bhurtpore Rajah's are good. The concourse of people to this city is astonishing. It is a great object of pilgrimage. Of course a multitude of Brahmins may be found in attendance, and the swarms of fakeers are immense. The disgusting nudity and gross impudence of the latter are extraordinarily offensive, though to us peculiar respect was shown. The account which Mr. Turner, the magistrate, has given me of the vice and bestiality of the fakeers is shocking. As the place is under his jurisdiction his information must be sure; and he is of too mild and conscientious a character to throw a loose imputation on any description of men.

February 14th.—We marched, and encamped about a mile to the east of Muttra. After breakfast I examined the ground, and had the satisfaction of finding it no less suitable to my purpose than the general position of the place is advantageous as a station for a division of troops which

I have meditated fixing here. Mr. Strachey, Resident at the court of Scindiah, met us here. He has told me that Scindiah was much perplexed, and evidently checked, by the rapidity with which we had collected force, but that his Highness did not appear alarmed, being satisfied that we should not break the treaty and attack him, unless he were guilty of some overt act against us. Mr. Strachey is deeply impressed with the conviction of Scindiah's mischievous disposition, and is persuaded he will not forego the opportunity, if serious reverses in the Gorkha war shall lay us under any embarrassments. That opening will not occur. We may not be able to achieve all that I could wish to effect against the Nepaulese Government; but I have taken care to furnish such plenitude of force in every quarter, that nothing untoward beyond simple failure in an object can take place. There is not room for anything disastrous; and accommodation may always be arranged with the appearance of superiority on our side. The remoter consequences of such a pacification would be deeply injurious; therefore every nerve must be strained to circumscribe the Gorkha power effectually; but

Scindiah has. let slip his time. Though he might still distress us severely, he cannot now play the stake without risking his own ultimate ruin. In the evening, I looked at the handful of infantry remaining here. The 1st battalion of the 1st Regiment made a good review. The new raised battalion of the 30th had not yet got its arms or clothing; but I was glad to see that the men were good and well brought forward in marching.

February 15th.—At the distance of about a mile from the cantonment, the land rises, and the level is then continued to an undefined extent. On that higher ground, I this morning reviewed the 1st regiment of cavalry commanded by Major Watson. It is in very good order, but extremely weak. The establishment of the cavalry is altogether too low. With the ordinary course of casualties they must soon dwindle to inefficiency in the field. In the middle of the day I went into the town. We were first led to the ghauts, which present nothing remarkable. Passing from them along a dirty, neglected path on the bank of the river, amid many cells of sanctity, and many filthy devotees, we reached the temple of Bul Deo. This is a

shrine of superior celebrity. The building, however, is poor. Though it is said to be very ancient,
I did not perceive in it anything curious in point
of ornament. A pair of coarse shawls and a bow,
which had been placed on the knees of the image,
were presented to me. It was intimated that this
was to be considered as a testimony of peculiar
respect. This hint was of course to regulate the
scale of the expected return. The latter appeared
quite satisfactory to the attendants of the temple,
who followed me, and begged that I would take
some little cakes of sugar to throw among the
crowd. We thence went to see a large mosque
which has fallen much into decay. It has been a
handsome structure. The front and minarets had
been gaudily decorated with enamelled tiles. The
colour of those which remained were vivid, and the
effect must have been pleasing while the patterns
were unbroken. I spoke to the magistrate about
some repairs to the edifice; not as to the minor
ornaments, which would be very expensive, but to
keep up the frame of the fabric; in particular, to
preserve the fine flight of stairs which led to the
court in front; suggesting to the magistrate that

the disposition of Government to contribute somewhat towards preventing the further dilapidation
of the building might, if mentioned, encourage
the Mussulmans to come forward and subscribe for
its restoration. I was answered that although they
had a bigoted attachment to their creed, they
would have no feeling to any proposition for repairing their place of worship. I have, indeed, observed with surprise the singular indifference which
seems to exist among the inhabitants of this
country, whether Hindoos or Mohamedans, with
regard to the condition of any edifices belonging
to their respective sects. I directed that what
was necessary for keeping the building secure
against the progress of injury should be executed.

February 16th.—Marched to Furrah; having
determined to take this route instead of the direct
line to Agra, in order to see the ruins of Futtehpore Sikri.

February 17th.—Encamped at Utchnara. The
country through which we have passed this day
and yesterday is populous and well cultivated. Mr.
Strachey had his hawks with him, and we had some

good flights at the *ibis igneus,* called here the
black curlew. Though upon near inspection the
feathers of this bird have a varying gloss of purple,
green, and gold, uniform black is the only colour
perceivable at a little distance; so that the Lin-
næan name affords a very inaccurate description.

February 18th.—Reached Futtehpore Sikri. It
is the ruin of a town which the Emperor Akbar
founded. His object was to have a residence in
the vicinity of good hunting ground, and he probably overlooked the consequence of collecting a
considerable population; namely, that the cultivation and communications which its wants would
produce must drive from its neighbourhood the
beasts of chase. This particular spot, one may assume, was fixed upon for the city on account of a
considerable abrupt elevation which offered an airy
position for the palace. This knoll is apparently
of the same quality with minor ones outside the
wall, whence the red stone of which all the edifices
are built has been quarried. The walls, which are
high and handsome, and flanked with towers at
proper distances, are of this stone. They exhibit
but little decay. In the afternoon we went into

the city. The passing through a gateway in good
repair, and then finding yourself in an extensive
waste of ruins, had an impressive effect. I know
not that I have ever felt the sense of desolation
more strongly. In every direction the heaps of red
stone testified that edifices of no mean class had
existed there, and must have been tenanted by
busy agents, though no descendants of such a population remained. We mounted the hill, passing
through the remnants of many gateways. Never
did I see buildings better calculated for duration
than those which surrounded us. They were constructed of large blocks of stone so carefully squared
that even without cement they would have appeared secure in their positions. The roofs have
been chiefly flat domes. All was solidity. Yet
these buildings are universally deserted, and most
of them ruinous. Having gained the summit, we
passed through two guard courts. The comfort of
the soldiery had been well consulted by a verandah
covered with a penthouse of very large stone slabs,
which surrounded the interior of the courts. Thence
we advanced to a building said to have been the
Emperor's private apartments. It is a tolerably

large, but not magnificent, square house, standing insulated. The choicest of the red stone (and those pieces appear as hard as marble) has been selected for this structure. In consequence, it shows no symptom of decay. On each side of the entrance door there is a stone covered with the interlaced triangles, the distinctive mark of the royal arch masons. These are on too large a scale, and hold too prominent a situation, to have been put in without permission by any of the workmen. I did not discover in any other part of these buildings, nor have I met elsewhere in India, a masonic emblem. The rooms within are small, and the staircases (for the house has two stories) are narrow and steep; and as is the case in all the buildings I have seen in this country, the walls are so massive that the residence was probably cool. No kind of hangings could have been used in the rooms, for they would have concealed the extraordinary labour, and indeed taste, with which the stones have been wrought. Many of the patterns and traceries are highly worthy of being adopted in our ornamental architecture. I took measures to have copies from the most striking of these.

The stables adjoining to this building are convenient, but without any aim at show. As much may be said of the hall of audience. A covered gallery by which the women were to reach a latticed turret or summer-house near the bottom of the hill is rather curious. It is not one flight of steps, but there is a length of passage, then a number of steps, then passage again, and so on till the descent is effected. The passages are supported by buildings which probably lodged servants. We returned to our camp much gratified.

February 19th.—We returned to the city, to visit a part where life and flourishing condition displays itself amidst devastation. This is an establishment kept up in honour of a Mohamedan saint. Cheisty Selim is buried there. A large landed estate is left, by the piety of successive emperors, to the saint's family, on the condition of their keeping up his tomb, and the buildings connected with it. The British collector, as a part of his public duty, looks to the state of these buildings, and gives due admonition to the family if any neglect appear. Thence everything is in perfect order. Winding through narrow paths,

among the heaps of rubbish, we came in front
of a noble portal. This entrance to the building
is truly magnificent, and is elegant also. Passing
through it, you find yourself in a vast quadrangle.
An arched piazza runs all round it, into which a
number of cells open. These are destined to lodge
devotees, who, at particular times, come in crowds
to prostrate themselves at the shrine. Above the
piazza there is a terraced walk, which, with a good
parapet, renders the building a place of strength.
From the top of the gateway tower the eye ranges
over a vast expanse of plain without a feature.
The tomb of the saint, within the quadrangle, is
surrounded by a light building, consisting of
beautiful screens of white marble, wrought to
imitate net-work. The effect is admirable. No
reluctance was shown by the Moslems to let us
approach as near as we pleased to the tomb. The
attendants took from it, and presented to me, the
muslin wrapper of a turban, some common-place
glass beads, some cakes of sugar, and a bow.
They took care to inform me that this was a
compliment only paid to sovereigns. Of course
my return of presents was to be proportioned to

this factitious measurement. The Rajah Rundhur Sing, of Bhurtpore, came and encamped within half a mile of us this morning. The failure of the British army, under Lord Lake, in different assaults on Bhurtpore (so circumstanced as that there was not a possibility of success), impressed the Rajah with the suspicion that there must be a rankling and irremovable animosity against him on the part of our Government, and some peevish differences between him and a magistrate of ours strengthened his notion that we must be in watch for the opportunity of striking at him. His vakeels, who had been sent to me with the ordinary compliments on my coming into the Upper Provinces, had been assured that none of that acrimonious disposition existed, and that their master would be received with perfect politeness, if he waited on me. The vakeels, from what they saw of our habits, were thoroughly satisfied that this declaration was sincere, and strongly urged their master to put himself on a footing of confidence by coming to me. Their advice prevailed. The Rajah asked leave to meet me, and this was the place appointed, as being the place nearest to his dominions. I have learnt that, as the hour approached, his fears began to stir a little, and that he has brought with him 5000 of his best troops, to secure him against treachery. There is no mode of correcting this spirit but by treating it with entire indifference; therefore, I did not allow my weak escort of one battalion and 100 cavalry of the bodyguard to appear to take any additional precaution. I apprized the Rajah that I would receive him at three o'clock, and he came accordingly, with a splendid and numerous suite. He was accompanied by Cooar Durjun Laul, his nephew and adopted son; by Cooar Madhoo Sing, younger brother of the former; by Foujdar Churamun, his minister; and by Foujdar Motee Ran and Dewan Jewahur Laul, the vakeels who had formerly been sent to me. Though I met him with frank kindness, his embarrassment was apparent. When he was seated, I resolved to apply a decisive medicine to his doubts. I professed my satisfaction at meeting him. I said it would be a gross injustice to the British character were any one to imagine that, from our having been foiled at Bhurtpore, we were capable of an unworthy sentiment towards those who had gallantly resisted us. I professed that we knew how to honour valour, though exercised against ourselves; that I rejoiced in making personal acquaintance with men who had so proved their martial quality; and that I would depend on their showing as much intrepidity by my side, if I solicited their assistance, as they had done against us. The relief which this tone seemed to give to all the principal persons was extraordinary. The Rajah became immediately cheerful and confident, pleasure beamed on the face of all his attendants, and we parted on a footing of thorough cordiality. I am sure he will sleep better to-night than he did last night. We had divine service at noon.

February 20th.—I went early to return the Rajah of Bhurtpore's visit. We found his camp and his tent of reception very well arranged. His manners were frank and exhilarated. He told me that if I wanted troops for any service, while I had so many of our own in the hills, all his were at my orders, and that he hoped I might find his cavalry at least useful. I smiled and said that there might be a contingency in which I should take him at his word.   I think he comprehended that I alluded to a rupture with Scindiah, for he said earnestly, "I would bring every man I have to you." We parted with at least this good done, that the apprehensions which might have, contrary to his wish and his interest, thrown him into a party adverse to us were eradicated.   The vakeels called upon Mr. Ricketts to tell him how happy he had been made by the language which I had held at my durbar yesterday.   It had, they assured him, banished every doubt from the mind of their Rajah; and they asserted solemnly that I might now depend on his troops if I chose to ask for them. It seems the poor man was so frightened that he had made another considerable corps advance to within seven or eight miles of us, to aid in securing his retreat.   In the afternoon I went to see a part of the palace which I had not examined on the first day.   It was the interior of the zenana.   Everywhere there was a profusion of carving on the stone, all well executed, and much of it affording useful studies.

In one of the courts, the pavement was inlaid with squares of black and white, to represent a

chess-board, so that the Emperor might make the
female slaves perform the moves of that game
before him and his Begums.   Thus in this life we
delude ourselves with costly and laborious prepara-
tions for amusements, in which we rarely, if even
once indulge ourselves when the arrangement is
perfected.   A detached edifice within this precinct
excites curiosity to define its use.   In the centre of
an octangular room a massy pillar rises; a balcony
or gallery surrounds the interior of the room at
about two-thirds of its height.   And from this balcony four bridges, with balustrades of marble
wrought in the network pattern, lead to the top of
the pillar, round which a similar balustrade is
carried.   It has been believed that a throne used
to be placed for the Emperor on this space, and
that he thence gave audience to petitioners.   This
seems wholly incompatible with the situation of
the building, which is within the precincts of the
zenana, and not concealed from the other apartments by any wall or intervening edifice.   It has
most likely been also the produce of ingenuity toil-
ing at resources against listlessness, and wasting
its efforts in inapplicable provisions.   One quits

this place with a mingled sensation of astonishment at the immense exertions to which the will of an individual gave rise, and of wonder that the perfected result of so much effort (extraordinarily calculated for permanency) should, in a comparatively short period, have been so utterly subverted. Among the mounds of ruins in different parts, I observed a number of large slabs, with much carving on them, lying neglected. I requested the magistrate to have them collected and sent down to Calcutta; prohibiting, however, the touching any which might retain their places in walls, although the buildings might be otherwise in thorough ruin.

END OF VOL. I.

CPSIA information can be obtained at www.ICGtesting.com
Printed in the USA
BVOW07s1645280214

346326BV00009B/339/P